Also by D. L. Kline

Suddenly Psychic

Clearing the Track

The College of Spiritual Knowledge

A Matter of Death and Life

Change a Letter, Change Your Life

Guidespeak

D. L. KLINE

Copyright © 2018 D. L. Kline.

All rights reserved. No part of this book may be used or reproduced by any means, graphic, electronic, or mechanical, including photocopying, recording, taping or by any information storage retrieval system without the written permission of the author except in the case of brief quotations embodied in critical articles and reviews.

Balboa Press books may be ordered through booksellers or by contacting:

Balboa Press
A Division of Hay House
1663 Liberty Drive
Bloomington, IN 47403
www.balboapress.com
1 (877) 407-4847

Because of the dynamic nature of the Internet, any web addresses or links contained in this book may have changed since publication and may no longer be valid. The views expressed in this work are solely those of the author and do not necessarily reflect the views of the publisher, and the publisher hereby disclaims any responsibility for them.

The author of this book does not dispense medical advice or prescribe the use of any technique as a form of treatment for physical, emotional, or medical problems without the advice of a physician, either directly or indirectly. The intent of the author is only to offer information of a general nature to help you in your quest for emotional and spiritual well-being. In the event you use any of the information in this book for yourself, which is your constitutional right, the author and the publisher assume no responsibility for your actions.

Any people depicted in stock imagery provided by Getty Images are models, and such images are being used for illustrative purposes only.
Certain stock imagery © Getty Images.

Print information available on the last page.

ISBN: 978-1-9822-1024-3 (sc)
ISBN: 978-1-9822-1026-7 (hc)
ISBN: 978-1-9822-1025-0 (e)

Library of Congress Control Number: 2018909605

Balboa Press rev. date: 08/13/2018

Contents

About the Cover ix
Disclaimer xi
Preface xv

Part I
December 18, 2013 3
Who, What, When, Where, and Why 10
Sing It, Kate 21

Part II
Islands in the Stream 39
Big 48
Whose Little Ism Is You? 57
Sphincter Boy 66
Time Passages 72
Build-a-Guide Workshop 79

Part III
James Earl Jones Is Not Your Soul Guide 87
The Elephant in the Room 98
The Universe Gym 103
There's Never a Bridge Too Far 112
Into the Woods 118
The Victory Lap 123

Preview of The Blueprint 127

For Pookie and Poodle,
ever and always

About the Cover

The cover art was done by an amazing artist and friend of mine named Stephanie Reigle. Even though she doesn't consider herself to be psychic, she is able to access the other side and let it direct her in her art to produce spirit-inspired paintings.

She had to endure Jasper, my soul guide (for which I apologized to her), telling her exactly how he wanted the cover of this book to look, and I think it turned out great.

He later told me that the artwork was meant to evoke the memory of the magic mirror that whoever the host of *Romper Room*—a children's TV show from my early childhood—would hold in front of her face at the end of every episode.

She would hold up the mirror with a sort of vortex on the back and say an incantation that included the words, "romper," "stomper," "bomper," and "boo," and some other words I don't remember.

Then she would say, "Magic mirror, tell me today, have all my friends had fun at play?"

The camera would cut away, and when it came back, we would be able to see her face through the magic mirror. She would then say, "I can see Davey, and Johnny, and Susie, and Mary," and a few other names.

Those of us watching at home would be waiting with bated breath to hear our names called, and then we would be thrilled if she actually called it because that meant she could see us.

The point of this story, which has turned out to be longer than I thought it would be, is that Jasper wants us to realize we should always have "fun at play" and not take life so seriously.

I couldn't agree more.

Disclaimer

It's very unusual for a book dealing with spirituality to begin with a disclaimer, I know, but the guides are pretty insistent that anyone who picks up this particular book understands what's going to happen as they read it.

I'm going to make a big assumption and think that if you're attracted to this book and its subject matter that you are progressing well in your spiritual journey and know—or think you know—something about soul guides. I'll also assume that you believe there is a lot to be gained, spiritually, by being able to interact with and hear from your own personal guides.

If you think you are the person I just described, then welcome in. The knowledge contained in this book is indeed written for you.

However, the warning part of this disclaimer comes from the fact that all spirit guides only speak the truth—no matter how hard it is for you to hear. They are incapable of deceiving or lying, so if you haven't or aren't ready to take a good long look at areas of your life that need work, the areas that keep you from unconditionally loving yourself, you're not ready for direct interaction with your guides.

Your guide sees you as an absolutely amazing and wonderful being, so if you're seeing yourself as anything less than that, it's going to be tougher to make a connection.

Once you get past the point of allowing and believing that your guides are indeed there for you and reach a place where you are comfortable hearing them on a regular basis, they are going to push your limits to help you fulfill the life plan you wrote for yourself.

Oftentimes, they are going to make you go to places in your subconscious where you don't want to go, and deal with lingering fears, anger, and guilt that you conveniently just tucked away instead of coping with.

Your guides only want the best for you. They are—and have been—with you through all of your many incarnations. They have a good understanding of the emotional baggage you have carried with you from life to life, and they want to do everything they can to help you resolve your issues so you can finally leave them behind and not carry them into your next incarnation.

If any of you have read any of my other books, then you are aware of my guide, Jasper. If you don't know him now, you will by the end of this book—intimately.

I think it would be safe to say that his methods of instruction are somewhat unorthodox, and he might even be considered the poster boy for using tough love as a teaching tool.

He gave me a few weeks' grace period in the beginning of our active partnership, but once that little honeymoon was over, the real

Jasper came through. He told me I was stupid in every imaginable way—and in some I never imagined—and he sometimes would go radio silent for days at a time.

In his defense, he acted exactly the way I asked him to when we were planning my current incarnation. We both knew I was going to be a pigheaded Pennsylvania Dutchman this time around, and anything less than being smacked between the eyes with a two-by-four, metaphorically speaking, of course, wouldn't have gotten my attention.

He did his job well, and as time has moved forward, we've become more and more connected, or more correctly, reconnected, so now he's rude and sarcastic just for fun, and only because I continue to find it amusing.

If you are afraid of what you're going to hear from your guides—or if you're hearing what your guides are saying, and it triggers a flood of negative emotions—then you are not ready to be in constant contact with them.

They will never lie to us like we lie to ourselves about emotional problems in our lives. They will never tell you everything is fine, just fine, when it's clearly not. They have no time to indulge us in the martyr role-playing that we're so fond of when we're incarnated.

As we move through this book, perhaps the scariest thing we are going to come to know, and one of the hardest ideas to grasp, is that our guides are actually us. We are them, and they are us. That makes us responsible for our own lives. There is nobody to blame for our problems but the person in the mirror. Horrifying, isn't it?

It's so much easier to blame god, or the devil, or your parents, or you third grade teacher, basically anybody who you think has made you feel the way you do, than to accept personal responsibility for how things are going.

Here's another scary news flash. You—and only you—are responsible for the way you feel from day to day. There is nobody on the planet who will "complete" you. Only you can make yourself feel happy. We're going to be talking a lot more about that subject down the road, so before I get too high on my soapbox about that, let's move on.

Our guides are pieces of us that we leave behind on the other side to help us during our incarnations. We do that because nobody in the universe knows us better than we know ourselves. They are best at seeing the inner workings of our puny human minds and using that information to direct us.

Remaining behind that amnesia veil that separates this dimension from the one next door, they also maintain constant access to the plan we wrote for our current lives, the better to guide us to our goals.

The last piece of this disclaimer has to include a warning about earthy language. Jasper, like all the guides, will use whatever he needs to get his point across, and on occasion, his language can get a little salty.

Now, growing up in the mountains of Western Pennsylvania, going to college in the 1970s, and working in health care for more than forty years has inured me to rough language. I think sometimes swear words are the best way to express what we're trying to get across. In addition, recent studies have shown that more intelligent people tend to swear more, something a lot of us knew all along.

All that aside, it's still kind of awkward sometimes hearing someone from the other side drop an f-bomb to emphasize a point. However, it will help you get over that whole seeing them only as angelic and celestial beings thing in a hurry.

So, there you have it. If you are easily offended, easily frightened, or don't like hearing the truth, turn back now.

If, on the other hand, you're ready to take a little thrill ride that could change your whole life, climb aboard. Please keep your arms and legs inside the moving vehicle at all times.

Preface

Over the past few years, it's become more and more apparent to me that there is almost no part of our spiritual journey that is as important as allowing, believing, and trusting in the existence of our soul guides.

The problem is, due to the things we learn in childhood from our parents and families about the universe at large, accomplishing those three things can be no small feat for some people.

If you aren't in a place of self-awareness that holds as truth the unconditional love of self, it can be very difficult to accept that there are beings in the universe who love you without condition and whose whole and entire reason for existence is to help you as you navigate your way through an earth life.

Even after you get to where you are accepting of yourself and the existence of your guides, there comes the next important step, which is being in contact and having conversations with them.

Once we reach the point where we are mindful of the positive effect they can have in our lives and know that they are able to point us in the direction we want to go, even the sky is no longer the limit.

Because our guides are living at home, or on the other side, whichever you prefer, they are constantly immersed in nothing but the positive energy and unconditional love that binds the universe together. The whole universe, that is, except for one tiny little exception: the earth.

This small planet where we've all chosen to incarnate is the only one, as far as I know, where negativity is the norm. Just as positivity and unconditional love are taken for granted in the universe at large, the earth exists as a showcase for negativity of every type and description.

It sounds like a bad thing, but it serves a very important purpose. It allows those of us who are strong enough and have a burning desire to incarnate here as many times as we choose to experience living in all that negativity. Only by doing that can we come to know it up close and personal, so to speak.

By living out a life in an atmosphere of nearly total negativity, and fighting not to become part of it, we learn coping skills that we carry with us through all our lives. Those coping skills make us spiritually stronger.

Soul guides have always been part of the equation when planning an earth life, but since the atmosphere of this dimension has become increasingly negative, their roles as the ones who can provide much-needed direction and encouragement has become exponentially more important.

Whether you call them guides, guardian angels or your higher self, or think of them as intuition or a little voice in the back of your mind, living out a successful incarnation without them would be nearly impossible.

Of course, as Jasper loves to remind us, because we only have access to about 10 percent of our intellect when we come here, many of us stupidly blunder around from a bad life scenario to a worse life scenario, thinking we can handle everything on our own.

That was the case for me for the largest part of my life.

In fact, after I got reacquainted with Jasper and my other guides, they thought it was hilarious that I had chosen to live the first part of my life with only minimal input from them.

After gaining direct access to them, I didn't think it was funny at all that I had kept them on the sidelines, but the whole thing was my doing and planning. I learned to cope with a lot of negativity while they were just watching events unfold. Everything happens for a reason.

Due to the ever-increasing need for people who have incarnated on earth to have access to and help from their soul guides, this book is going to delve more deeply into the who, what, where, when, and why of guides, bring about a better understanding of how to communicate with them more effectively, and illustrate how they can help us once we do.

Along the way, we're also going to be looking in more depth at those three ugly stepsisters—anger, fear, and guilt—and how they can hinder the free flow of information between us and our guides.

When we choose, and make no mistake, it is a choice, to hold on to anger, fear, and guilt for long periods of time without trying to get to the bottom of why we're doing that, and more importantly, trying to deal with those negative emotions to get rid of them, we can block nearly all communication from our guides.

They simply can't reach us when we are focused on negativity, especially when it applies to how we feel about ourselves.

Our guides know we are totally amazing beings for even deciding to come here in the first place, but they have no way to reach us if we are in a constant state of self-doubt and self-loathing. At those times, it's like we only understand and speak Mandarin Chinese, and our guides only understand and speak Greek. There may be some gesturing and pantomiming as an attempt at communicating, but there is no real understanding on either side.

My goal, along with all the guides on the other side, is to provide enough information in this book to get everyone in direct contact with their soul guides on a daily basis—just as I am with mine.

I hope yours will be a little more compassionate and understanding than mine. Since they act the way you instructed them to while you were doing the planning for this life, you can't complain. Whatever it is, you brought it on yourself.

I can't wait to get started—so let the adventure begin!

December 18, 2013

I couldn't possibly—and Jasper certainly wouldn't let me—begin a book about soul guides without relating the epic saga, his words, of how I met and opened up to my guide. He and I have the sort of relationship that allows us to call each other many different names, not all of them fit for mixed company, but most of the time, he is Jasper.

December 18, 2013, was the memorable day when I was finally able to see him and talk to him directly, even though he had been with me since I was born, as all our guides are with each of us. So, seven days before Christmas in the fairly unremarkable year of 2013, I got the best gift I could ever hope for: the grand entrance into my life of my BFF, Mr. Showbiz, or J for short.

Let me backtrack a little for those of you who have not read any of my other books and give you the entire story of how this Christmas miracle happened for me—or *to* me. I'm not sure which yet.

I had always had a passing interest in so-called psychic phenomena, but for the first sixty years of my life, that's about all it amounted to. I had attended psychic fairs occasionally and had seen some mediums on television, but I was too busy living out a fairly normal life with work and family obligations to deeply pursue any of that type of knowledge.

Then, through a series of coincidences I had planned out before I came into this life, I met my friend, the amazing psychic and healer Barb Ruhl, to do some past-life regressions.

I know a lot of people do past-life regression as a therapy, hoping to unlock things from their past lives that might have been held over and are causing them problems in their current lives. That is a valid reason to do regression, and sometimes pinpointing in your subconscious the origin of a problem from a past life can help people deal with it in this life.

I, on the other hand, just wanted to see if I had any past lives, and I thought it would be great fun to experience those lives if they were there. And it is an unbelievably fun thing to do!

It's very much like going to an amusement park and leaving your current reality behind, especially if you can find a skilled and connected regressionist like Barb. I had a few sessions, and Barb and I poked around in my subconscious, visited nine of my many past lives, which had occurred over about four thousand years of human history and covered territory ranging from the deserts of ancient Egypt to the jungles of South America and everywhere in between.

It was all a great adventure, but as our friends on the other side like to say, just reliving pieces of our past lives may be lots of fun, but we are here to live and learn from our current incarnations. Basically, they were trying to nicely say, "Quit fooling around and get back to work!"

After we had closed the door on the ninth of my past lives, Barb said, "Hmm."

By that time, I had known Barb long enough to understand that when she says "Hmm," she is hearing or seeing something really interesting.

I said, "What?"

She said, "They are telling us we can see another dimension."

"What does that mean?"

"I don't know. I've never heard that before."

I said, "Cool, let's go!"

Unfortunately, our session time was up, so we had to wait until our next appointment.

The next time we met, Barb immediately said, "There's an energy here who says his name is Jasper—and he will be guiding us on our tour."

That's when I first was able to see him, and that energy named Jasper has completely changed my life.

I think a lot of people have the impression that their soul guides are equivalent to what they picture as angels: white flowing robes, glowing faces, and maybe even wings and a halo.

If envisioning them that way works for you, that's great. You can and should expect to see them exactly the way you think they should look. They really don't care how or even if you see them. The only thing that matters and is truly important is that you trust and believe they are there, seen or unseen.

In my first encounter with Jasper, I really didn't have any expectations about his appearance or how he should or could act.

My ignorance about soul guides turned out to be a very good thing because when I first saw him, he looked to me exactly like the cartoon guy on the Little Caesars pizza box. He had the large nose, the laurel wreath, and the black hair—and a little bit of an attitude.

I'm happy to report that, as my connection to the other side got stronger and my vision got clearer, he came to closely resemble Al Molinaro, the actor who played Al from Al's Diner on *Happy Days*. Jasper's image has settled now to being like a younger and better-looking Al Molinaro, but he's kept the same general appearance.

I once asked him why he looks the way he does because I never had any great connection to *Happy Days*, and his answer was that all great character actors, which he considers himself to be, have offbeat looks so that they can adapt themselves to any role that they are required to play.

Honestly, folks, this is what I've been dealing with for the last few years. I'm pretty sure for this incarnation, he kept about 99 percent of our self-esteem for himself because he has no problem at all acting like he has a shelf filled with Golden Globe and Emmy awards at home.

And would I trade him out for another guide? Not for all the tea in China, as my dear grandmother used to say.

Despite all his name-calling and making fun of my puny human mind, he is exactly the type of energy I need to get and keep my attention, kick my butt when necessary, and keep me moving forward in my spiritual journey.

Why does he act the way he does, and why is he exactly what I need? Because I planned for him to be the way he is before I incarnated this time. I knew that by the time he was able to get through my thick Pennsylvania Dutch skull, I would be in such a rut and so set in my ways that if he wasn't over the top and sometimes loud to the point of being annoying, I would simply have ignored him and pretended he wasn't there.

He made it almost impossible for me to not know he was there, and he has encouraged, berated, pushed, pulled, prodded, admonished, and greatly amused me since he came into my life. I wouldn't have it any other way.

It's more correct to say since I realized he was in my life. He's always been there; I just wasn't aware of him.

Along the way, as the great thespian he says he is, he has assumed the personas of everyone from Liza Minelli to Humphrey Bogart to Ginger Rogers to Ringo Starr as the conductor on *Thomas the Tank Engine*. He has been a cowboy, an astronaut, a Christmas angel, a belly dancer, and a fisherman—just to name a few of the roles he has played recently.

Why does he go to such lengths to get his point across? Because, all else aside, he is my teacher for this incarnation, and the way we have things set up, I learn best when he can reference an old movie or television show. It makes whatever he is trying to tell me very relatable for me, and to be honest, it makes it a lot easier to describe and write about all the things he is trying to teach all of us.

Two of his most recent star turns have been as Kate Smith singing "I Saw You Last Night and Got That Old Feeling" when he was trying to tell me why people in general, and me in particular, waste so much time rummaging around in their old subconscious memories and as Patsy Cline singing "Walking after Midnight."

He changed the lyrics of the Patsy Cline song to ones that may or may not be suitable for mixed company, but we'll get into that in a later chapter. For now, let's just say they relate to working hard at keeping our minds open in order to be receptive to information from our guides at all times.

That particular chapter will be titled "Sphincter Boy," and I may have to give it a PG-13 rating, but sometimes the other side will use some coarse or harsh language to grab your attention if they think it is necessary to make you pay attention to what they want you to hear.

They will always tailor the delivery of the message to the individual, so if you are easily offended by that type of language, they will find another way to communicate.

Being from the mountains of Western Pennsylvania, I grew up hearing, shall we say, earthy language, so not much shocks me. In fact, I usually think it's funny because—like a lot of grown men—I still retain pieces of my twelve-year-old-boy sense of humor. Jasper knows he can use whatever language he chooses, and it won't bother me.

Other than being a constant source of entertainment, how else has Jasper changed my life? First and foremost, with him around, I am never—and can never be—alone. I grew up out in the country, and the common thread that runs through my childhood memories is loneliness. That's not always a bad thing, but too much of it can make you a sad and sorry person.

Again, it was all part of my life plan, but being unaware of the internal connection we all have with the other side can change simple loneliness into feelings of isolation.

Knowing and being connected to Mr. J has forever resolved that issue. In fact, sometimes when he pops in at two or three in the morning to tell me something, I start wishing he would shut up and wait until morning. That's when I start longing for some of that solitude of my youth.

Secondly, he was the one who told me I had to start writing books to share everything I've been experiencing with the rest of the world. It was just a coincidence that it would let the rest of the world meet him too, I'm sure.

In all the sixty years I lived before I met him, I never had the faintest notion that I would write a book, and the quality of writing in my first books proves maybe I shouldn't have, but I've improved with his help.

Before he came into my life, I really didn't have much to write about. He provided the drive to write, and he provides most of the material I write about.

Third, he is the greatest teacher I have had in all my eighteen years or so of formal education. I think I can say that without offending any of my former teachers because I think most of them have transitioned by this time, and I'm sure I wasn't always the greatest student.

Anyway, his methods, which most would not consider mainstream, are perfect for penetrating my puny human mind.

Maybe, above all else, he serves as my constant connection to the other side.

In fact, Barb and I recently realized that our guides are always only on the other side. We both had thought that when we are in direct contact with them, they come to us. In fact, the exact opposite is true. They live permanently and only in the positivity and unconditional love of home. In order for us to be in close contact with them, we need to raise our positive vibration to a level where they can meet and communicate with us.

And that can take a lot of work and a lot of time.

I don't think there is anything special about me personally, other than the dramatic turn my life took at an advanced age, but I do believe that the way I met Jasper may be rather unusual.

I only say that so no one gets discouraged when they are trying to contact their guides and it doesn't happen right away. They are always there and ready to talk to you, but many of us have issues we need to work through before direct contact can be established.

In other words, you may have a corporate logo pop into your head someday and start giving you advice, like I did, but it's probably not going to happen that way. The vast majority of people are going to have to take a lot of baby steps toward their guides before they actually get to the place where they are always accessible.

But not to worry! The whole purpose of this book is to give you the knowledge and skills you need to do just that. Let's get started with the who, what where, when, and why of soul guides.

Who, What, When, Where, and Why

Who, what, when, where, and why are, of course, the aptly named 5 Ws. These five basic questions are the foundation of a number of disciplines, ranging from scientific research to journalism and law enforcement.

The reason they are so useful in such diverse fields is that none of the questions can be answered with a simple yes or no. By asking one of the five, you get the maximum amount of information about whatever has piqued your interest with just a one-word query.

For our purpose, which is having a fuller and more complete understanding of the five Ws concerning our soul guides, I'm going to give you the best answers I can to those questions.

These are the answers the guides provided for me.

I didn't want to trigger (no pun intended) any outbursts from Jasper, but he just popped in looking like Mr. Ed and singing, "Go right to the source and ask the horse—he'll give the answer that you endorse."

I know you've already figured this one out, but he's saying we'll be getting our information straight from the horse's mouth. That way, it will be as accurate as it can be when transmitted through an imperfect filter, which is me.

Only a few paragraphs into the new chapter, and we're already being treated to a floor show from J. Now he's Barbra Streisand singing, "How Lucky Can You Get?" from *Funny Lady*. Will the entertainment ever stop? Please?

I hope he can keep it to a minimum—or else this book is going to end up being the length of *War and Peace*. He says he doesn't care because there will finally be a book that is all about him.

Moving on. There are three qualities that anyone who wants to have a closer relationship with their soul guides must possess: allowing, believing, and trusting.

Even though I list them separately, they are closely intertwined.

You first have to allow that there are such things as soul guides, and then you have to allow yourself to believe that they exist and that you can have one or more. Then, you have to trust that belief and trust that they are there and helping you get through this mess called life.

Allowing, believing, and trusting are the things that must be present in order to build a relationship with your soul guides. However, before you can lay that foundation, you need a thorough understanding of exactly what you are putting your faith in.

Let's start with the first of the five Ws and answer the who question.

Before we incarnate for a life here on the earth plane, as I have written about many times, we make extensive and detailed plans for those lives in order to give ourselves the best possible experiences for learning to cope with multiple emotional scenarios and enhance our soul growth in the process.

During and after all that planning, we are never separate from the presence of the pieces of our energy that we have designated to be our spirit guides.

The term *spirit guide* means just what it says: part of us will be remaining in spirit, or at home, whichever you prefer, and they will be the part of us that has constant access to the life plan we wrote for ourselves.

Our amnesia about life on the other side prevents us from seeing our life plans directly while we're incarnated.

Recently, the guides have been saying that they actually prefer to be called "soul guides" because it more accurately portrays their function.

It also sounds a little less "new agey" than spirit guides. We see them as spirit guides because they live in what a lot of people think of as spirit, and they are providing guidance for our soul's journey from there.

Either term is correct, but I didn't want there to be confusion if I switch back and forth going forward.

Because our guides have detailed knowledge of everything we are hoping to accomplish during our incarnation, and if we are open to hearing them, they can try to nudge or point us in the right direction to keep us on that plan.

If we get distracted and start to drift away from it, they can get us back on track, thus accomplishing the "guide" part of their titles.

There is nothing magical or mystical about them, even though Jasper just appeared dressed as Mickey Mouse from *The Sorcerer's Apprentice* to let me know he can, indeed, be magical if he wants to be. I think we're all aware of that by now, Mr. J., but thanks.

When they are in human form, it's comforting for many people to think of guides as angels or some other type of celestial being.

However, guides are parts of our own personalities that we either won't be using a lot during this incarnation—or they are pieces of our personality that we want to experience a human life without just to see how that would feel.

In most cases, they will be the emotional opposite of how you have chosen to be in this life. The yin to your yang, if you will.

I think for a better understanding of the who and what of soul guides, I will be using Jasper and how he and I interact as an example.

I am basically a quiet and shy type of person, and Jasper is the exact opposite, being very outgoing and loud. My friend Barb, on the other hand, has a very bubbly and friendly personality, and her guide, Ella, is the soft-spoken, no-nonsense type.

Both Ella and Jasper dovetail perfectly with Barb's and my individual personalities to make a more rounded persona.

In *Jerry Maguire*, Tom tells Renee that she "completes" him, but there is no one here on earth that can make us "whole".

When we and our guides are connected, we make that "complete" person that being with someone on earth can't possibly accomplish.

We are always complete beings, but only 10 percent of what we are can incarnate here. The other 90 percent stays home.

In my case, Jasper holds most of our self-esteem because I masochistically wanted to see what it would feel like to go through a life always feeling a little "less than" everyone else.

Now that he and I are in constant contact, he's letting my feeling good about myself seep back in, so that we can improve our connection through the unconditional love we share. But more about that in a later chapter.

There are at least as many soul guides as there are people currently incarnated on the planet, but that number may be falsely inflated by Jasper's many costume changes.

Everyone on earth has at least one, and most people have two or three. I personally have six, and Barb has nine. The number of guides may increase or decrease proportionally to the complexity of the life you planned for yourself. Regardless of how many you see, they are all different aspects of your personality. They and you still make up one whole.

The total number of spirit guides is in the billions, and they are a common occurrence, but don't be fooled into thinking they can't do uncommon and extraordinary things. In addition to doing everything they can to help us fulfill our life plans, they are sometimes able to manipulate things on the earth plane to prevent us from going totally off the rails.

I can think of at least four times in the past fifty years when I could or should have been killed or severely injured in a car accident but came away with only minor or no injuries.

I wasn't aware of it at the time, but now that I have an all-access pass to Jasper, he told me that he was able to move the vehicles around in my car accidents just enough to prevent my being killed so I could do the work I'm doing now.

The most recent occurrence was just last winter. I hit a patch of black ice, and just when I was sure I was heading into a bridge abutment, the wheels got traction—and I was able to steer away from it.

I still drive by that spot on my way to work, and if I'm not thinking of anything in particular at the time, he will remind me that he saved my life there. Of course, I'm eternally grateful and not just because I'm eternally reminded of what he did for me.

But I digress. Back to who and what soul guides are. I mentioned that I have six guides, so let me tell you a little about them.

I met Jasper first, of course, but not long after I did, he took me to a place that looked like a long hallway with a set of bleachers on one side. The seats were occupied by five cartoonish-looking characters, and they were cheering and saying, "Yay, he's getting it back. He's getting it back!"

I later found out they were referring to my psychic abilities.

After my "vision" improved and I could see Jasper as a real person and not a cartoon, he took me back to that place, which turned out to be a very nice room containing six impressive red leather chairs in a theater-style configuration of three above and three below.

Five of the chairs were occupied by the rest of my team of guides. They told me their names were Jennifer, Judy, John, Julius, and Joe.

Why do all their names begin with the letter J?

Jasper said, "We all thought it would be fun this time around to do that and call ourselves the J-Team. You know, like the A-Team, but in the tenth-best position."

Of course, his name also starts with a J, so they are his team—not the D team—even though their purpose is only to help me. Allegedly.

Just kidding, of course. They are there to help me during this incarnation, but since he's the spokesman for the group, they are his team too.

As time has gone on, I realized that I was rarely seeing anyone but Jasper anymore. It's not that my other five went away or were killed and had their bodies hidden by him (I don't think). It's that he can give me all the information I need without the bother of contacting multiple sources.

It seems that when people choose to have multiple guides, one will be chosen to act as sort of an interpreter for the rest.

When one of my other five guides has some advice to give during one of my life scenarios, they will transmit it to me through Jasper to prevent confusion on my part about where the message is coming from. My puny human mind is easily confused, which he loves to remind me about.

I guess since we're still in the who and what section of this chapter, it would be a good time to talk about something that people on this journey sometimes get obsessed about, which is the names of our guides.

First of all, when we're at home, we don't really have a need for names because everybody knows who everybody else is by their vibrational energy.

Secondly, if you've lived a hundred different lives here on earth, then you've had a hundred different names. How would you single out which one you want to be called? Third, and maybe most important, our guides couldn't care less what we call them.

The late, great Sylvia Browne met her spirit guide when she was a teenager. She didn't like the name her guide told her, so she immediately decided to call her Francine, which was how she referred to her for the rest of her earth life.

And, as I said above, Francine couldn't have cared less. Being connected is all that matters.

I introduced all six of my guides previously, but let me tell you a little about each one.

You already know Jasper, probably too well, but he is basically the gang leader and my primary teacher. John is a serious, no-nonsense guy. He refuses to assume any kind of human form, and he just stays in an orb shape because he thinks looking human just to fit in is silly. Joe is all business, but not like a stuffy Wall Street banker. He is more like a laid-back, Silicon Valley executive. Julius appears as an older and wiser energy, and he has a lot of good advice to dispense.

As for the ladies, Jennifer is very bright and bubbly, with an almost fairy type of energy, and Judy is a strong, confident woman, the kind always played by Rosalind Russell in old movies.

They sound like a very diverse group, and they are, but they symbolize pieces of my personality that I didn't bring with me for this incarnation. I left them on the other side for two reasons.

First, our human bodies, while necessary to keep all the pink squishy stuff inside while we're alive, are very confining, and our puny human brains can only contain so much information, making it necessary to bring only the essentials.

Guidespeak

Secondly, and luckily, we don't need 100 percent of our personalities when we come here. We only bring those parts that we feel are necessary to accomplish whatever goals we've set for ourselves in our life plans.

It's like packing for vacation. If you're going to the beach, you don't need to take ski boots and a parka. You only need a bathing suit, sandals, and sunscreen; you don't have to drag everything you own with you.

Also, depending on your life plan, you shift the number and personalities of your guides around to provide you with the maximum support needed for any given incarnation.

If I were to incarnate as a female, I might shift Jennifer or Judy to spokesperson, much to Jasper's dismay. Doing that would allow them to help me through scenarios that are particular to women. Things like childbirth (help me, lord) or having to cope with male stupidity.

If I am more of a business person, I might shift Joe or John to the spokesperson role, and if I am to be a teacher or sage, it might be Julius.

You get the idea. Since guides are there only to help you maximize the learning you get from the life plan you have devised, you mix and match them before you incarnate to get the biggest bang for your buck. I think I may have let a little of John or Joe come through in that last sentence!

I guess the who and what of guides could be boiled down to the simple statement that they are you, or more correctly, pieces of you that you keep on the other side during your earth lives as sort of a reserve of knowledge and an emergency backup to your main soul guide in case you need help in their particular area of expertise.

After that exhaustive explanation of the who and what of spirit guides, the where and when are going to seem rather simplistic.

The where of guides is easy to understand because they exist only in the positive atmosphere of unconditional love on the other side. They can extend their energy to the earth plane to physically do things here, as Jasper did to move cars around to keep me from bodily harm, but the bulk of their energy has to remain at home.

We're going to go into that in much greater detail in a later chapter, so I'll just leave it at that for now. The other place they make their presence known is, of course, in your head.

This might be a good time to talk about your guides being in your head.

Even though I often write that Jasper said this or Jasper said that, I've never actually heard his voice. I'm not sure he has what we on earth would consider a voice. It's more like he inserts what he wants to say into my brain as a thought or a memory of what was said.

Since you and your guides are part of the same whole, their voices, if you do hear them, will be the same as your voice.

It's the same with their appearance. I may write that Jasper looks like Carmen Miranda in a tutti-frutti hat, but I don't actually see him with my eyes. I have the thought of seeing him that way in my head. Does that make sense?

Your guides' appearance and sound will be more like thoughts that pop into your head than anything you actually see or hear.

When anything Jasper says requires an answer, I may or may not reply out loud, but my response will more than likely be in the form of a thought.

When we're at home on the other side, all communication is telepathic, but in our physical bodies, we're used to verbal communication, so it's okay to talk out loud to your guides if it makes you feel more comfortable to respond that way. Just don't do it in public unless you have your cell phone handy so you can pretend you're on it with someone.

All activity in the brain is in the form of electrical energy that can be measured in a number of ways, including electroencephalograms, so it makes sense that beings that are composed of vibrational energy—as we are on the other side—would use it as a form of communication.

That pretty much sums up the where of guides—so let's tackle the when of guides. This one is also pretty easy because, since they are you, they are always with you whether you hear them or not. The when is from the day you are born until the day you transition home.

The guides are saying that, for some people who don't incarnate frequently, their guides may join with them as soon as they transition home. They become one energy.

For people like me who start planning to reincarnate almost as soon as they get to the other side, the guides will stay as separate energies and rearrange themselves as required to be of the most use during the impending incarnation. To sum it up, your guides are wherever you are because they are you and you are them.

Finally, we come to the age old and most FAQ. Why are there spirit guides at all?

There are a number of answers to that question. First, they exist because you exist. Second, they exist because you need them to help and advise you while you incarnate here for an earth life. Third, they exist to be repositories of the pieces of you that you leave behind on the other side. Most importantly of all, they exist to be your connection to the unconditional love of home. Having the strongest possible connection with your guides should be the primary goal of all of us on this spiritual journey.

As Jasper says, "Connection brings all good things." He's been on a kick lately of providing me with little sayings that he claims I should have embroidered on pillows.

He's trying to tell us that if we get to a place where we can unconditionally love ourselves enough to make a good connection, they can reflect back enough unconditional love to keep increasing the strength of the connection.

This forms an unending circle of love that can make our earth lives a whole lot easier to endure.

I think we've just about covered the 5 Ws of spirit guides for now. Your guides are more than happy to answer any number of questions 24/7—even Jasper! In case he is getting close to going into "grumpy-dad" mode and telling me to go ask your mother, we better move on.

Sing It, Kate

They're probably aren't a lot of people out there who remember Kate Smith. For those of you who don't, let me save you a Google search and provide some background information.

According to Wikipedia, Kate was a great American entertainer who transitioned home in 1986 after a fifty-year career in show business. She was the queen of radio in the 1930s, and she also starred on Broadway.

Kate was famous for singing "God Bless America," especially before Philadelphia Flyer hockey games, where her performance often proved to be a good luck charm for the team.

She had a lot of hit records over the years, but we're particularly interested in the one with the following lyric: "I saw you last night and got that old feeling, when you came in sight, I got that old feeling … once again I seemed to feel that old yearning, then I knew that spark of love was still burning."

I know what you're thinking. What could a lyric from the 1940s sung by a woman who passed over thirty years ago have to do with our spiritual journey and our guides?

Well, if you can simmer down for a minute, I'll tell you!

One of the most important things we have to learn to do in order to strengthen our connection to the guides is stop looking at all the old crap we keep around that reinforces all the feelings of anger, fear, and guilt we have accumulated in this and our past lives.

Jasper popped in as Kate Smith to sing that particular song because the lyrics are so fitting for this subject. We like to get "that old feeling" about our bad memories, and there are times when we actually feel a spark of love for them and yearn to go back to the place where we keep them.

Jasper tells us to knock it off.

Nothing can be gained spiritually by rummaging around in old memories unless you're doing it to finally deal with all the negativity in them. When you are just looking at them for the sake of looking at them, you are basically on emotional autopilot. It's much easier to wallow in those old memories than to try to deal with them and get rid of them. If you are in love with your feelings of fear, anger, and guilt—especially fear—you'll never be able to see or feel anything different.

Your subconscious thinks it is protecting you by running the same old programmed behavior over and over. It will keep doing that until you can provide a new program to replace the old one. The only way to do that is to release all of the fear, anger, and guilt that we insist on holding onto.

The problem is that, according to the law of attraction, we manifest into our lives whatever we're paying the most attention to. You can't move forward in your spiritual journey if all you see around you are old ways of thinking and behaving.

To get a better mental picture of what the guides are trying to teach us, imagine your mind as a house. It can be any kind of house you like, but for our purposes, it's probably best to see it as a big, old Victorian with an attic you can walk up into and a big basement.

Most of our lives are spent on the first and second floors, just going about our daily business. We're often not consciously aware of the things we have stored in the basement and the attic.

However, once you decide to embark on a spiritual journey, and realize you need your guides to help point the way, it becomes extremely important to bring the contents of those two places into your daily awareness.

See the attic as full of all the good things you want to remember: boxes and trunks full of positive memories and valued souvenirs from your current life and all of your past lives. The attic also represents your crown chakra and is closest to the vibrational level of your guides.

The basement, on the other hand, is a dark and dank place that is also full of boxes and trunks.

These containers are filled with all the negative emotions that you and your subconscious decided to hold onto and cherish instead of realizing they don't add any positivity to your current life.

Your subconscious can also keep you from dealing with them by putting them back in the trunks and boxes and duct-taping those suckers shut.

Your subconscious lives by that old saying: Better the devil you know than the demon you don't. It would be very happy if you never changed your way of thinking about any of your negative life scenarios because it knows how to react to them.

It feels it is the safest thing for you if you just keep walking the well-worn path you have been on because any change in your reactions to your fear, anger, and guilt could lead you in a more positive direction, and it doesn't know what new and different emotions you might encounter there.

That is why change can be so difficult. You have to convince yourself that the positivity will be better for your life, and you have to convince your subconscious that you will be emotionally safe on the journey.

You can make things a little easier by letting your subconscious rummage through those old memories and then discarding them as not relevant to your life as you move forward.

To make it even easier, instead of looking at each individual past negative scenario and judging its worth, tell your subconscious that whatever its holding onto is no longer relevant to your new life. It needs to lock all those trunks once and for all.

Once again, have one of my favorite *Wizard of Oz* moments, do a Glinda the Good Witch, and say, "Be gone—you have no power here" to all those wicked old memories.

What do we gain by keeping that cellar full of boxes of crap anyway? Why would we want to go down there and rummage around in the smelly, moldy things?

Are we just "wookin' pa nub" in all the wrong places like Eddie Murphy sang as Buckwheat on *SNL*?

As we just discussed, the things stored in your basement in all those trunks and boxes are the memories of negative emotions from this life and all your past lives.

All those memories are kept by your subconscious as examples of contrast because you have to see and know what you *don't* want before you can see and know what you *do* want.

We often get so attached to how easy it is to not think about that contrast that we end up not changing because the negativity is the only thing we truly know and trust.

My boxes and trunks—Jasper says it's mostly trunks—were filled with anger and guilt until I embarked on my spiritual journey in a real and determined way.

I subconsciously loved being angry, and I would revel in it on a daily basis. It was the perfect excuse for me to act like a jerk. I could use my anger to justify almost anything from treating other people badly to acting out at work.

I loved to hold on to my anger so much that I think I mentally installed a ramp to the basement so I could send the storage boxes down there faster. Once that ramp was installed, it was harder and harder to find the stairs to get the hell out of the cellar. I began to spend more and more time down there with my beloved negativity.

By spending so much time wallowing in your fear, anger, and guilt, it becomes difficult to see any of the positivity in your life. Constant fear promotes spiritual inertia, and constant anger promotes victimhood.

Those two bad guys play off each other and can cause spiritual paralysis. There is no introspection or self-examination if you are constantly blaming other people for how you are feeling emotionally.

I can't even pinpoint exactly when I bottomed out emotionally. I just remember thinking at some point that I was exhausted.

It takes a great deal of energy to be angry at everybody and everything all the time, and I got to a place where I was really sick and tired of being sick and tired, as the old saying goes.

It was then, without actually knowing it or identifying him as a separate entity, that Jasper started whispering in my ear and helped me change the direction of my life.

If I had an angry outburst, the voice in my head would say, "Are you proud of that? Do you really feel better now?" He would even ask, "Happy now?" I knew I wasn't.

Jasper helped me find the stairs so I could come up out of the cellar and start to live on the first floor of my life again.

I wasn't quite ready to go to the attic and meet him directly because I still had so much fear, anger, and guilt inside of me that it took some time to work on it and get myself to a place where I had enough self-love to let him guide me more directly.

Looking back now, I see how he manipulated the circumstances that led to my watching that *Montel Williams Show* where I first saw Sylvia Browne.

I just happened to be off work that day, and the TV just happened to be tuned to a channel I rarely watched. Seeing Sylvia and hearing her connect members of the audience with transitioned loved ones was the starting point of my spiritual journey.

Jasper, as well as most people in contact with the other side, can tell you without a doubt that there are no such things as coincidences. There are only cleverly disguised signs pointing us in the right direction. It can take years to learn to deal with all of your stored-up fear, anger, and guilt.

Don't expect things to change overnight, but you might be one of those lucky few who can learn all this faster than I did. If so, you might progress more rapidly than I did.

The boxes and trunks in the basement are filled with all the crap we manifest so easily, but that *doesn't* mean we have to go down there and rummage around when we're feeling insecure about where we're headed. Trust that your guides will show you the way to the attic and help you get there.

Even though I can say with pride that I haven't been down in my cellar for some time, a memory connected to fear or anger pops out of my subconscious every once in a while.

When that happens, I ask Jasper to put on his Igor from *Young Frankenstein* costume, bundle up the bad old memories, take them back to the basement, and throw them in one of the trunks.

When I hear a lid slam shut, I can rest assured that I won't have to deal with whatever that mess was for quite a while. Luckily, Jasper loves role-playing so much that I never have a problem getting him into any kind of costume.

But I digress. As I said before, when I got to a place where I was sick and tired of being sick and tired, 24/7, I decided I needed to change.

I don't know if there was a specific incident where I realized I was embarrassing myself, but I definitely knew I was getting to an age where I had a good chance of having a heart attack or stroke if I didn't get control of my negativity.

A large part of the letting go was realizing and accepting that I was responsible for my own emotions. It's not your family, your kids, your spouse, your boss, the other driver, that clerk in the grocery store, the government, or anybody else who is making you angry.

You are making yourself angry by the way you respond to how other people act.

Nobody is making you scream at your wife and kids. You're doing that all on your own. Nobody is making you swear and honk your horn at other drivers. You are doing that all on your own.

You are the only one who can be held responsible for your emotional outbursts. Claiming that you are only reacting to how someone else acted is falling into feelings of victimhood, which is one of our favorite things to do when we come here to live out a human life.

Is not getting angry at some jerk who cuts you off in traffic one of the hardest things you'll ever have to learn? Absolutely. It was for me, but I learned to handle that situation by looking at it in a whole different way.

Instead of getting angry, screaming, swearing, and flipping off the other guy, let him go in front of you, think, *If that's what he needs to do to make him feel better about himself, then he must have a sad life*, and let it go.

Do you think he cares what you think about him or whether he is making you angry? I can guarantee you he does not. All you are doing is wasting a lot of your energy on someone who doesn't care what you think and can't even hear what you are saying about him.

That is just a small example of how you can start to get rid of some of the anger in your life, but it is an important one because it's something we all can relate to.

It's always best in matters pertaining to your spiritual journey to start with baby steps, and not losing your mind while in traffic is one of the smallest steps you can take.

I can still hear you saying that I talk a lot about releasing fear, anger, and guilt, but how do you actually go about doing that? That is an excellent question because it has an easy answer.

You make a conscious decision not to get angry. It's that simple.

If you're reading this book, I have to assume you've come far enough along in your spiritual journey, that you are in touch with your feelings, and that you can tell when you're starting to get angry.

So just don't. Don't let yourself get angry. Stop yourself when you feel it coming on. Don't allow it to happen.

I can also hear all of the "yeah, buts" starting to fly. If you truly want to move forward on the positive spiritual path you want, the one that you, in fact, planned for yourself before incarnating, you have to make that road a "yeah, but-free zone."

You can't say, "Yeah, but that idiot just cut right in front of me." So what? If you're really serious about letting go of anger, here's one place to start. Don't get angry about what other people do.

The only behavior you have absolute control over is your own. Take control—and don't let yourself get angry.

I've also found that it helps a great deal if you can avoid the things that trigger your anger.

First, you must identify them.

For example, if you get upset and angered by things you see on the news, stop watching. Personally, at news time, I change the channel to some retro station and watch something like *The Love Boat* or *T. J. Hooker*. It's always entertaining, and it's usually good for a laugh.

Your life will go on, and it might actually improve without knowing the most recent thing some politician said or did. In the grand scheme of things, it really doesn't matter that much.

The same thing applies to social media. If you have that "friend" or two who keeps posting political opinions that contradict yours, just unfriend them. Remove the negativity that you know can set off your anger.

Once you've spent some time on introspection and figuring out exactly who and what you are angry at—and eliminating those things as much as possible from your life—you are going to start to feel so much better about yourself, your life, and the world at large. It will be noticeable to you and the people who are close to you.

Once you can feel that difference, you'll be able to sense your guides more fully. They will be able to give you inspired actions to take to point you in the right direction.

While you're waiting to see the changes in your life that your hoping for, you can fake it 'til you make it.

I'm not a huge fan of that phrase because I don't think you should fake anything in life, but by using it, the guides mean you should start feeling the way you want and expect to feel when your life improves—even if that hasn't happened quite yet.

If you make yourself purposely feel joy and expectation while you're waiting for a change, there is no room for you to feel anger, fear, or guilt. There will be no place for them in your new belief system.

You have to get yourself to where you believe that what you want is coming. You can't just kind of believe; you have to absolutely and unconditionally believe that things are going to change in the way you want them to.

As hard as it may be to do, you have to remember what it felt like on Christmas Eve when you were about six years old. You didn't know exactly what was going to be under the Christmas tree in the morning, but you had faith that it was going to be something great—and maybe even something that had been on the list you gave to Santa at the department store.

We need to channel those same feelings of anticipation and excitement into our spiritual lives.

Even though, as adults, we won't know exactly when that thing we want is coming, or even what form it may take, we have to capture that emotion of expectation we had as little kids on Christmas Eve.

That was a time in our lives when we unconditionally believed that good things were going to be provided for us. As adults, we too often put so many conditions on what we want that our guides can't possibly bring it to us.

We have to allow the process to work organically without placing who, what, when, and where conditions on getting it.

If you say, "I want a million dollars in my bank account by Friday morning at ten," most likely it's never going to happen. And when it doesn't happen, we put on our favorite sack cloth and sprinkle the ashes, and we blame the universe for not giving us what we asked for.

The best course of action is to let your guides know that you would like to make more money and then let them show you how you can do that.

I don't know if it was the influence of a recent Super Bowl, but when I was having some doubts about how things were progressing in my life, Jasper showed up dressed as a football coach with a chalkboard covered in x's and o's and arrows running in every direction.

When I asked what any of that had to do with what was going on in my life, he said he was the coach, and he holds the playbook containing the plan for this incarnation. He would be calling in all the plays that needed be run, and I should just relax and watch the game.

Once again, emphasizing trust that your guides can see a bigger picture than you can and are handling things the way they should to make things move forward.

Kiss Me, Kate was an old MGM musical that starred Kathryn Grayson, Howard Keel, and the amazing tap-dancing feet of Ann Miller.

Jasper is so excited about this movie reference that he can't even decide which part he wants to play. He says he'll just play them all.

One of the songs from the movie is a tune called "We Open in Venice," which is about the opening of a traveling show. "We open in Venice, we next play Verona, then on to Cremona, lotsa laughs in Cremona."

The words are really unimportant to what we're talking about, but the catchy little tune is what matters for us. Unfortunately, there is no way to let you experience it while you're reading. If you want to hear it, you're going to have to visit Mr. Google or actually watch the movie. If you haven't seen it, you should watch it anyway. It's a classic that will further your cultural education.

But I digress. If you have the tune in your head, you can replace the lyrics with the words that have been provided to me by you-know-who: "I trust you, now show me. I trust you, now show me. I trust you, now show me. I believe, then I see."

If you're in the market for a mantra to use while meditating, Jasper says this is the perfect one. This direct dialogue with your soul guide says that you allow and believe they are there, that you trust that they are there to help you accomplish your goals—even if you're not exactly sure what they are—and you are open to allowing them to send you signs and signals about which way to go.

It also ends with an affirmation taken from the law of attraction: When I believe, then I see. It's all wrapped up in a neat twenty-three-word package.

One of the most frequent questions about help from your guides is, in the words of Whitney Houston, "How will I know?" How do I know it's actually my guide putting ideas into my head? How can I be sure it's not my imagination? What if I'm just going crazy and hearing voices?

These are all valid questions, so here are some tips on ways to separate your own thoughts from conversations with your guides.

First, don't expect to hear any voices but your own. You and your guides are pieces of the same whole, so they will sound like what you think you sound like.

Second, your guides see you as an amazing, perfect being, and they will never speak to you from anywhere but the unconditional love they have for you. There will never be any negativity in their communication—with some rare exceptions to that rule. We've already talked about how Jasper is not above using tough love if he thinks I need it.

Third, they possess and hold at all times the plan you made for this life. Even if you have lost sight of your learning goals, they will be able to nudge you in the direction you need to go to fulfill your plan. Even if it doesn't seem so to you, everything they tell you will be relevant.

How do they do all these things? They can do it in very subtle ways, which is why you need to be as connected as possible to them.

You might get a feeling to read a certain book or newspaper article and see an opportunity. You might get an urge to watch something on TV or YouTube and learn something that will help move you along.

I once got a feeling that I should check my spam folder in my email, something I rarely do, and I found an opportunity there that I would have completely missed out on had I not been prompted to look.

You might be part of a conversation where someone says something that is completely out of context, and you get the feeling that they didn't even know what they were saying. It's another way your guides can send you a message if you need to hear something out loud.

You may overhear part of someone else's conversation and realize what you heard was meant for your ears.

I have visions of all of our guides sitting around on the other side with a handbook of ways to get messages across to their humans and going down a checklist: "If that doesn't work, try this. If that doesn't work, try this."

It's lucky that they do love us unconditionally and that they live in a dimension where linear time doesn't exist. Otherwise, they would just throw up their hands and walk away in frustration at our being so dense and oblivious to the help they're trying to provide.

My dear BFF is not above using tough love when he thinks I need it. In fact, he recently gave me his list of the seven levels of human consciousness that we all pass through on our spiritual journey. It is as follows:

1. moron

2. dolt

3. lunkhead

4. idiot

5. dunce

6. clueless

7. dazed and confused

I'm proud to say I have passed through the first five stages.

According to him, I am hovering at about a 6.5, where I range between clueless and dazed and confused. That does not prevent him from occasionally demoting me back down to lunkhead, or even dolt, albeit temporarily.

This is why I laugh when people tell me they want to have a spiritual experience like mine and a guide like Jasper.

No, you really don't. He's my burden to bear, and everyone has already written their own personal spiritual journey.

What they mean is that they want the very close connection I have with him, and that is possible for everyone. It just takes time, effort, and the old ABT: allowing, believing, and trusting.

In the next part of the book, I'm going to be describing many examples that Jasper has provided to illustrate the interactions that can bring us closer to our guides.

I hope one of them will make sense and turn on a light bulb for someone. Maybe they all will—and that would be great.

Before we go on, Jasper has a personal message for everyone on the next page.

Stop!

Jasper says, "You may think you have an understanding of all the things you just read in the first part of this book, but you don't! Go back and read it again—and then you can move ahead to part II. You might even graduate from dolt to lunkhead!"

Islands in the Stream

This part of the book, the middle section, is structured to present many different views of the guides, in the hope that one of them will strike a chord with as many people as possible.

We are all on our own individual vibrational levels, spiritually speaking, so sometimes when one explanation doesn't sound quite right or doesn't ring a bell, another one that is worded in a slightly different way will bring an a-ha moment.

Because of our puny human minds, it can take a lot of guide 'splainin' before we finally grasp what they're trying to teach us.

The reason I'm giving you information that might seem discouraging about this part of the journey is that I know from personal experience what it's like to feel like a dunce—and then to be actually called one by your soul guide.

Remember Jasper's list of levels of human awareness? On any given day, all of us could be at any level on that scale, depending on how well we are perceiving what our guides are trying to teach us.

I am not different or special in any way, but I am in constant and close contact with my guide, so if it can take me some time to figure out what he's trying to tell me, it can take the average person a lot longer.

Don't beat yourself up because the answer to your question or the lesson they are giving you isn't exactly clear at first. It takes a lot of time and effort to be maximally connected to your guides, so give yourself a break if it doesn't happen right away.

Okay, enough gloomy forewarning. Let's get to the topic at hand: ways to envision your guides.

The title of this chapter, "Islands in the Stream," is taken from a great old song by Dolly Parton and Kenny Rodgers. The lyrics this time around don't have much to offer in the way of illustrating the concept we're talking about, so we'll just focus on the title.

Jasper says to think of your current earth life as being a floating island in the stream of passing time.

Or, more correctly, think of the life you believe you want to live as being on that island.

The problems arise when we feel like we're trapped on the shore, looking across the water at the island, and not knowing how to get over there.

The water looks deep and treacherous. We're pretty sure there are sharks swimming in there, and to top it all off, it seems like the island is moving around.

We aren't even sure we'd be able to swim far enough to get there without drowning.

And who is putting all those negative thoughts and ideas in our heads? Who holds on to all our fears and is more than happy to throw any or all of them at us if it looks like we might be serious about changing how we view the world?

The answer to that question is looking back at you in the mirror.

We, in the form of our subconscious, are the most adept at sabotaging any forward spiritual progress because nobody knows or loves our fears more than we do.

Though I often vilify the subconscious mind, the truth is that it is neither a good or bad influence. Keeping you safe from harm is its primary goal. The problem is that it can only attain that goal by keeping everything in your life exactly the way it is.

Even if you are miserably unhappy, your subconscious feels comfortable and safe there, so it doesn't want you getting any big ideas about changing anything to make yourself happier.

It thinks that if you try to improve yourself in any way, you might fail, and then on top of being unhappy, you would be hurt and sad as well. If you just stay where you are emotionally, you won't run the risk of living with more pain.

Is any of this ringing a bell with anyone out there? It should be extremely familiar to all of us because this scenario is the source of the fear we all encounter when we start thinking about changing our emotions in order to advance on our spiritual journeys.

When we get to a place where we can recognize that our fears are being generated from within ourselves, we've taken a huge step forward.

At that point, we're starting to emerge from the mass of people who are wandering around in the forest by the aforementioned stream.

Unlike the majority of them, we can at least stand on the shore and see and know there is an island out there where we'd like to be.

We're beginning to recognize that the life we truly want is on that island, and the inhabitant of the island who can help us move toward that life is none other than our soul guide.

Even with the knowledge that there is something more out there, we're still stuck on the shore, trying to figure out the best way to get over there.

It's never easy, especially at first, to believe and trust your guides unconditionally—there's that word again—but doing both those things is the key to getting yourself to that island.

How do you go about it?

Erase those old fear-based programs that your subconscious wants to keep playing and replace them with a new program based on believing and trusting.

Guidespeak

The hardest part of getting your subconscious to change its ways is replacing those old programs that have been playing in the background for your entire life because it thinks they are keeping you safe. You absolutely need to have replacements ready and waiting to download before you can get it to toss out the old ones.

Allowing, believing, and trusting in your soul guides is the perfect way to do that, and your guides can actually help you.

Once you have 100 percent trust in them, even if you don't think you are hearing them, they will show you positive things by sending you inspiration that will give you a feeling to try this certain thing, do that certain thing, or look over that way and see what you can see.

They will always be doing whatever they can to move you forward. They will never suggest anything that feels negative in any way, which is one of the ways you can figure out if it's them or your own thoughts coming through.

If you see yourself standing at the water's edge, still a little fearful, and you get the inspiration to stick your big toe in the water just to see how it would feel, that would be coming from your guides.

Let's say you stuck that toe in, and it feels good. The water is warm and calm, and it's a nice experience, so you decide to wade in farther. When you look up, it seems like the island is moving closer to where you are.

Now you're thinking, *This is cool. What exactly was I was afraid of?*

If you've dealt with your subconscious negativity, the answer should be: "I can't remember."

With no fear holding you back, you dive in and start swimming toward the island.

The problem that arises with most of us at this point in the journey is that—thanks to our old programs—we think, *This seems too easy. How can this be so simple? I don't deserve this.* That's when the sharks of doubt start to appear.

You stopped trusting for a brief time, and your old friend the subconscious starts playing your fear programs.

Suddenly, you're floundering. You start thinking, *If I had stayed on the shore, I would be safe right now.* The sharks start circling, and it looks like the island is farther away than ever.

Don't worry. All is not lost. It's just a matter of stopping, taking a deep breath, and consciously recommitting to trusting and believing in what your guides are trying to tell you.

Since they are a part of you, if you're not trusting them, you're not trusting yourself. You have to believe that you can make whatever meaningful changes you want to make in your life.

Your guides will be there to help you all the way. Listen as they say, "Yes, it can be this easy. Yes, you are deserving."

No matter how much you are doubting yourself, it's important to stop treading water and start swimming. You can't make any progress without making the effort to move forward.

There will still be times when you have to stop and catch your breath. You may even be swimming in the wrong direction occasionally, but just like those sharks you were afraid of have to swim to breathe, you have to keep moving to stay spiritually alive.

Your guides will always be there to give you all the help they can, but you are the part of the whole that is here and incarnated. It's up to you to do the heavy lifting and actually keep things physically moving.

Right or wrong, you are always in charge of the direction you're moving. Trust in the guides to make sure it's the right direction.

After struggling and flailing for a time, which is perfectly normal, you make it to the island. Congratulations! Now what?

This whole exercise has been a metaphor about getting in closer connection with your soul guides, which is the point of everything we're trying to accomplish on our spiritual journeys.

The island in our story represents the other side, or the dimension next door, as some people refer to it. It's the place where our guides live while we are here on earth for our incarnations.

And why is it so important that we go there, not physically, but spiritually?

Because, unfortunately, our guides can't come all the way here to meet us. We have to go to them. They only live and function in the state of unconditional love that exists on the other side.

And how do we change our vibrations enough to get to where they are?

By mastering all that fear, anger, and guilt that dwells in our unconscious minds, we can raise our spiritual vibrations to the place where our guides can lower their vibrations enough to meet us.

Sounds easy enough, right?

Wrong. It's not supposed to be easy. If we could be in constant and effortless contact with our guides, then what would be the point of coming here in the first place? We could just stay home and enjoy their company 24/7.

We come here to play this game of life because it is a challenge and never a gimme.

Even though I'm sure there are some teenage computer wizards out there who can master any new video game in a day, how is that any fun? You want the game to be complicated and messy, not easy, so you have the desire to keep playing.

And that is how we want our lives to be, whether we want to believe it or not.

Even after making it to the island, you may find some fishhooks stuck in your clothing, and they may be attached to lines that are pulling you back toward the water.

The fishhooks are little reminders to us that even though we think we have it made, there may still be some lingering and nagging fears that our subconscious may be using to draw us back to what it considers to be our "safe place."

To get this far along, most of us will have conquered nearly all of our fear, anger, and guilt.

However, a huge fear that might remain is the biggest fear faced by those of us who choose to go on this journey: the fear of not knowing if or how we and our lives are going to change once we start growing spiritually.

Will I be a different person? Will the people around me still like me? Will *I* still like me? These are all valid and concerning questions, brought about by our inherent fear of change.

Luckily, the answers to all of those questions are simple. First, since the goal of going on any spiritual journey is to change from a person living in the negativity of fear and anger to someone living with a positive outlook on life, if you don't become a different person, you're doing something wrong.

You may lose some people from your circle of friends and relatives when you start changing your outlook on life and your vibration, but once you get yourself to a more positive place, people with the same positive outlook will be there waiting for you.

You may actually welcome the opportunity to leave some of your more negative friends behind because negative people love to dwell in their own negativity, and you'll find that being with them in that place just doesn't feel right to you anymore.

As you become more and more connected to your soul guides and feel the unconditional love they have for you, your love for yourself will go through the roof.

It's much easier to love everyone else around you when you have love to give because your soul is filled with it.

Above all, those so-called fishhooks should only be viewed as minor distractions. They can easily be removed and thrown back in the water so that your subconscious will no longer have an attachment to use to pull you backward and away from your forward progress.

The information in this chapter may be new for a lot of people, so take as much time as you need to digest it all. To sum it up, let me repeat some of the important points.

Our guides only experience a human life through us, the incarnators.

They are not human, and since they sit in unconditional love, they can't have any human emotions or shortcomings. Their positive energy doesn't tolerate negativity. That's why they stay on the other side, and it's up to us to raise our positive vibration levels enough to go to where they are.

Each time we incarnate, the guides we choose during our life planning have a slightly different persona than in our previous lives. We do that to maximize the amount of help and guidance they can give us in each new scenario we will be encountering.

The number of guides you choose to have can vary with each life and from person to person. Having more guides than other people doesn't make you special or important; it just means you've put in as many as you think you will need to match the challenges of the life you have planned.

The persona of your guides plus your persona equals the totality of who you really are. If you were to separate your guides from each other, you would see that they reflect all the facets of your personality.

Having a number of different guides allows our puny human minds to see them as having different personalities and sort them out by their individual traits.

As we're going to learn in the next chapter, it's almost impossible to comprehend how big we are in a universal sense when we are incarnated in these small physical bodies.

Finally, every time we incarnate on this planet, we plan to be more spiritual than the last time. Unfortunately—or fortunately, depending how you look at it—the negativity on this planet and the human experience itself can cause changes to that plan while we're living out our earth lives.

But just in case things work out the way we actually planned them to, our guides are standing by to keep pointing us in the right direction.

Always remember that you control your guides. They don't control you. They can only point, nudge, and encourage if you ask them to.

Above all, you have to trust that they are there to do whatever it takes to give you the life you planned for yourself.

Big

Jasper told me a while ago that it was time to work on making myself bigger. Of course, my first thought was, *Awesome, let me run to the store to stock up on Little Debbies.*

That earned me a big eye roll from him, and he explained that I really needed to have a better understanding of the fact that there was more to me than the physical body I currently occupy—a lot more.

He meant that I needed to make myself spiritually bigger with his help. I was doing a fine job of making myself physically bigger all on my own.

He wanted me and everybody else who is incarnated for a life on this planet to know that we only bring about 10 percent of our totality with us when we come here, which means about 90 percent of who and what we truly are remains at home on the other side.

When we're there, at home on the other side, we have no problem with knowing for certain that we are limitless beings because we can plainly see and experience that we are connected to, and part and parcel of, the universe at large.

Jasper and all of our guides know it's nearly impossible for our puny human minds (his words, not mine) to fully comprehend that this person we recognize as ourselves is only a small piece of what we actually are.

Some of that is by design, so that we can learn and grow from the struggles we face during our incarnations, and some of it comes from the fact that we impose an amnesia on ourselves while here so that we have only fleeting memories of what our real lives are like on the other side.

If we truly remembered how great our lives are at home, we would all be joining hands and jumping off of bridges, as the late, great Sylvia Browne used to say.

When we decide to incarnate here and stuff as much of our real selves into these very confining physical bodies as we think we'll need to live out this incarnation, we lose all perspective about the reality of our normal size.

Just as very valuable things here on earth are often referred to as priceless because there isn't enough money in the world to buy a replacement, at home, we would be considered size-less because we can literally be the same size as the universe.

I realize this is a very abstract concept. Our puny human minds have a tough time processing and comprehending it while we're living within the limitations of our present incarnations, but I think it's important to have as much of an understanding of it as we can.

It's only by making ourselves as spiritually "big" as possible that we can fully take advantage of all the help our soul guides can give us as we move forward in our journeys. Our connectedness, if you will, to them only improves when we begin to understand the totality of who we are.

Once we get an idea of our actual spiritual size, even though it's a great thing to know, we shouldn't become focused on what parts of us are here and what parts are there.

Jasper says it's less relevant that we know what the 90 percent of us that we leave behind consists of because it can lead to feelings of not being complete or not having the tools we need to successfully live out an incarnation.

It's more important just to have the awesome feeling of knowing a huge part of us is not here, but it is available to us if we fully reconnect with our guides. When we start feeling small, insignificant, or alone, we can use the knowledge of our real size to tell ourselves that we are none of those things.

We are eternal and universal beings who are living one current life out of an infinite number of lives in this one small body.

Jasper says to think of it as a slice of pizza—not a slice of some frozen excuse for a pizza from the grocery store, but a big, cheesy, greasy slice of real New York-style pizza from your favorite pizzeria.

Picture the slice hanging with the pointy end down. That little tip of the slice with the gooey cheese hanging from the end represents you during an earth incarnation, including the grease.

The rest of the gigantic slice of pizza is the part of you that remains behind on the other side so that it is not subjected to the corrupting influence of all the negativity on this planet.

What's the takeaway from being compared to that melting drop of goo on the tip of a really good slice of pizza? Even that little bit of goodness is connected to the rest of the slice, and it all works together to make the entire thing fabulous and delicious.

We are never alone on our individual journeys. We may feel abandoned by family and friends, but our soul guides are always with us—whether we feel we are in contact them or not.

Perhaps even more importantly, through our guides, we are always connected to the biggest and best part of ourselves.

After we have an understanding of how we fit into the universe, or maybe more correctly, how the universe fits into us, what can we do to maximize ourselves while incarnated? How do we imagine filling out the form of what we believe our true selves to be? How do we wrap our heads around having separate parts to our personalities?

Let's take a trip to the movies and think about a great picture from the 1970s starring Sally Field titled *Sybil*.

According to Wikipedia, the movie was based on a book of the same name. The author lived in New York and, due to her abusive childhood, developed sixteen different personalities that all manifested at different times.

The movie and subject in general are way heavier than the glitzy and glamourous show biz references Jasper usually likes to use as a teaching tool, but he chose it to illustrate that we all have a certain amount of split personalities going on. We just have to realize it and use it to our advantage.

Consider our past lives. We've all been everything possible at one time or another. Each of us has been man, woman, gay, straight, indifferent, all of the available skin colors, rich, poor, you name it.

We've all had at least one life with each human variant in order to get an understanding of what it would be like to have that certain kind of experience you can only have by being all the different variables possible.

That's not the kind of split personalities we're talking about. Those personalities all existed in totally different physical bodies and in different locations and time periods.

We're talking about you in this particular life and the way you decided to divide up your entirety before you incarnated this time. Since we spend a great deal of time planning each life before we incarnate, we can use all the details in those plans to decide what character traits will be of most use in accomplishing our goals this time around.

To make this concept a little easier to understand, lets think about packing to go on vacation again.

With the high cost of checking luggage on an airplane, we all try to pack as lightly as possible.

Because space is limited, you only want to take what you absolutely need, and the same applies to what we bring into our physical bodies when we incarnate.

What you bring with you can have a big impact on how well you learn what you want to learn. That's why you put a lot of thought into what you're bringing before you come.

I left most of my self-esteem at home with Jasper this time because I apparently wanted to learn what it would be like to try to function without a lot of it and then learn how to get at least some of it back. Why anybody would do something like that is a question I frequently get asked.

The answer is to learn—as simple as it may sound.

It's not a test if you have all the answers. And if it makes you feel any better, you're never allowed to plan anything into your life that you haven't attained a spiritual level that would give you enough emotional tools to deal with the scenario.

We bring the pieces of us that we think we're going to have the most need for when we incarnate, and the rest of us stays behind in the form of our soul guides.

This might be a good time to talk about the number of soul guides we all have.

Obviously, you and your guides combined make one whole being, but the first time I actually saw my guides, there were six of them, including Jasper. Barb has nine guides, and when I have seen other people's guides, there are usually three.

Why all the varying number of guides? When beginning our spiritual journeys, our puny human minds can't handle the thought of being connected to and reliant on only one otherworldly energy.

When I first saw my six, they all had very different personalities. It was a comfort to know that I had all those souls connected to me and there to help me get through this earth life.

I already described the whole gang in detail, so I'm not going to go over it all again.

As I grew in understanding of how the universe functions, and how all the parts work together, all my guides merged into Jasper. I rarely see the other five anymore. It doesn't mean that they aren't still there, but it's not necessary for me to see all of them all of the time.

It could also mean that I've gotten lazy to the point of not wanting to worry about identifying which one I'm talking to at any given time.

Maybe I'm content to have Jasper be the spokesman for the group. There is no need to obsess about how many guides you have or don't have.

Having more guides than someone else does not make you special in any way. It just means that wherever you are in your spiritual journey at any given moment, you have the correct number of guides in place to give you the most amount of help when necessary.

Our soul guides are adaptable energies that can change themselves to be how and what we need them to be according to both the course of our spiritual journeys and our particular stages in life.

When we're young children, our guides often appear as imaginary playmates and relate to us on a level we can understand at that age.

As we grow, the guides morph and change to be however and whatever we need them to be. Just like the room of requirement in the Harry Potter books, they will appear when we need them in whatever form we need them to take.

If you're more comfortable with thinking of your guide as an angel, or some other celestial being, they have absolutely no problem appearing like that for you.

They love you completely and without condition, and they want you to be successful and accomplish all that you planned for yourself. For those reasons, they are willing to do whatever they can to help you better see them, hear them, and accept their help and direction.

And then there are those few of us who have chosen guides like Jasper. It's not that I don't know that he loves me unconditionally. He does—even though I don't always make it easy for him. It's just that some of his caring is shown in the form of tough love, which I'm sure I wrote into my life plan one day when I was feeling particularly masochistic.

As an example, I know it's my fault for not being able to break my addiction to the word "when," but I'll be absolutely sure he told me that something would be happening by such and such a date.

If that date comes and goes with no changes in sight, I'll be depressed and angry and ask him what went wrong.

That's when he'll tell me to think back. Do I really remember him giving me an actual date?

Of course, the answer is no. He never gives me firm dates for anything because too many variables can come into play. I just think that things should be happening, and then I blame him when they don't.

Unfortunately, I've put myself through that scenario on more than one occasion. I recently learned a big lesson about changing the "when" in my vocabulary to "whenever." I'm hoping I finally learned what he was trying to teach me so it doesn't happen again.

But enough about my personal issues. Let's move on to another movie, and this one is not nearly as depressing as *Sybil*.

About twenty years ago, Tom Cruise made a really good movie. It's not that he hasn't made good movies before and since, but this particular one has a line of dialogue that is of interest regarding how we relate to our soul guides.

In *Jerry Maguire*, he says, "You complete me."

I know it sounds romantic and all that kind of stuff, but if you don't feel like you can be a whole person unless you have a significant other in your life, you are probably so needy that you will never be able to attract said other in the first place.

The lesson we're supposed to be learning from this movie relates to how our soul guides are an integral part of us, and we of them.

Despite the things we were taught to believe in our formative years, like that ever-present feeling of not quite measuring up in so many ways, we are all complete and wonderful beings.

If you combine the 10 percent or so of our consciousness that we bring with us when we incarnate and the 90 percent or so of us that we leave behind, it always adds up to 100 percent. We, as humans, plus our soul guides, always equal the totality of who we really are.

Looking back to the beginning of my own spiritual journey, Jasper looked like the guy on the Little Caesar's pizza box. From the get-go, he has always had this thing about using pizza as a metaphor for what our consciousness resembles when we incarnate.

His obsession may stem from the fact that we both view pizza as one of nature's perfect foods. The other one is Little Debbies Swiss Cake Rolls.

He suggests thinking of one of your life goals as trying to shove a giant piece of pizza through a mail slot.

At first, only the pointy end fits through—and only for a short distance. By trusting our guides and allowing them to help us in any way they can, we can actually enlarge that mail slot to allow more of the slice to come through, giving us greater access to more of the wisdom and knowledge we left behind.

I don't know who said it first, but I believe Wayne Dyer said it best when he wrote, "We are not human beings having a spiritual experience. We are spiritual beings having a human experience."

It's great to have people in your life to love—and who love you back—but combined with our soul guides, we are whole entities. We don't really need anyone else to "complete" us.

Unfortunately, without increasing the connection between us and our guides, we can spend the bulk of an earth life looking for love in all the wrong places. We never find the greatest love of all: the love of self.

Hey! I think just I came up with two great song titles in one sentence!

Whose Little Ism Is You?

Who doesn't love Carol Burnett? Even though today you mostly see her comedic genius in snippets on infomercials, I was lucky enough to be able to see her television show when it was broadcast in the 1960s and 1970s.

Many people aren't aware of it, but according to Wikipedia, she actually started in show business as a Broadway star. She starred in the original *Once Upon a Mattress* and was a featured performer on the Garry Moore Show. Somewhere along the line, I remember her singing a song about a glass prism titled, "Who's Little Ism is You."

I readily admit that I'm not extremely tech savvy, but when I went searching for the lyrics to this song, I came up empty. In this instance, I think Mr. Google may have failed me.

Ordinarily, I'm a huge fan of Mr. Google, and I have spent more than a few hours going down internet rabbit holes provided by him. However, I couldn't find any information about the song or its lyrics. Either the lyrics are very obscure, Carol never really sang it, or I just imagined the whole thing.

Guidespeak

I was shocked. I have never had a question that couldn't be answered by Mr. Google—even if I had to change the wording in my question several times to get where I wanted to go.

At that point Jasper, ever the educational opportunist, decided to step in with a timely lesson about communicating with our soul guides.

In an unusual departure for him, he appeared as himself and not as some Hollywood star from days gone by. Granted, he was in his favorite attire, a Roman toga, but that's his default everyday costume, so I hardly notice it anymore.

His message for the day was to think about how Google works. You have to enter the right words, usually in the right combination, to get the answer you're looking for.

Jasper has told me many times that computers on earth are patterned after the way communication works on the other side, so it's not by coincidence, I'm sure, that getting the answers you want from your guides works in exactly the same way.

If you feel like you've been trying and trying to get the answers to the questions you ask of your guides, and the answers just aren't coming, it could be that you're not asking in the right way or with the right combination of words.

Sometimes your guides can't give you a direct answer because they would reveal too much of your life plan, and that is a big no-no.

Other times, it might be that you left explicit instructions with them to not make things too easy and to let you puzzle things out on your own.

The biggest reason they may not be answering your questions comes from the fact that they are 100 percent unconditional, and if you are asking using the five Ws we talked about in the first part of this book, you will rarely get a direct answer because you're putting conditions on what you want to hear from them.

Nothing puts more conditions on getting an answer from them than continuously asking when, where, why, who, and how.

I refer to them as the five Ws even though *how* starts with an H, and I consider them all four-letter words—even though most of them have three letters.

All of them need to be banished from your spiritual dictionary and your *Guidespeak* vocabulary, but *when* is the biggest offender. It's my Achilles heel, and it has caused me more than a little emotional turmoil from time to time.

By using those words to ask things like, when, where, and how will something happen, especially when talking to your guides, you are reinforcing the idea that something is lacking in your life and that you're being deprived of something that should be in your new reality.

As we learned when we studied the law of attraction, if all you can focus on is what's not here, what you want to be here will never appear because what you are focused on is the lack of what you want.

In one of his more helpful suggestions, Jasper said, "If you find yourself stuck in that place where you know what you want, but you're frustrated because it hasn't happened yet, it's time to put your guide goggles on."

For those of you who are country music fans, I'm sure you know what beer goggles are. For those of you who are not fans, beer goggles magically appear after you've had a few too many beers, and having them on makes everything around you appear wonderful.

Life is suddenly really good because you're looking at the world with your beer goggles on.

Jasper says the same thing can work for those of us on our spiritual journeys. If you don't like looking at your current scenario, put on your guide goggles and look at it from your guides' perspectives.

You can do that by moving your thinking to an unconditional place as much as possible, and you can start by adding an "ever" to the end of all five of the Ws.

In changing your thinking in that one simple way, *what* becomes *whatever*. "What's it going to take to get me to the reality I want to see? Whatever! I'll do whatever I need to do to get me there, and my guides will show me the way."

"How will I get there? However! I don't know exactly how I will accomplish what I want to, but I know I will do it, and my guides will be showing me what I need to see."

"Who will help me? Whoever! My guides will, of course, but they may send other people into my life to give me nudges in the right direction as well. The more, the merrier."

"Where am I going to find the help I need? Where am I going to end up? Wherever! You think you may know exactly where you want to go, but you may have planned something completely different for yourself. Guess who has access to your life plan? That's right, your guides, and they are going to point you in the right direction."

And the most conditional of all? When. "When will I get what I want? Whenever! Whenever all the conditions are right for me to get it." I know these changes in wording sound like Valley Girl answers to serious questions, but that kind of attitude is exactly what you need to adopt for this part of your journey.

Constantly asking your guides when, when, and when will only slow things down because you're putting earthly time constraints on them.

They are the ones who have the long view of how your life is playing out, and they are the ones that are moving all the levers and pushing all the buttons behind the big curtain, just like the Wizard of Oz in the original movie.

They also have complete access to your life plan, which allows them to align all the cogs in the gears of your life machine so they mesh together at precisely the right time to let things unfold as they should. You have to absolutely trust that they are going to do just that.

Stop working so hard at trying to force things to happen. Let your guides do the heavy lifting. They already know what you want out of life, and even better, they know how to get it for you.

Become an entirely new creation, a redneck Valley Girl. Put on your guide goggles and say, "Whatever!"

Jasper thinks it would be great to make "Redneck Valley Girl" T-shirts. It's a thought.

You thoroughly planned this life before you came here—so relax and sit in your happy place while your guides take care of everything.

Always remember that you are your guides and they are you. If you don't trust them to handle this, you're not trusting yourself to have planned the life you wanted to live to learn what you wanted to learn.

Jasper just showed up dressed as Bob the Builder to emphasize the point that he and all of our guides are, first and foremost, able to build the lives we want for ourselves because they hold the blueprints we left with them before we incarnated.

And also, like most men, he really enjoys wearing a tool belt.

Wow! Talk about going down a rabbit hole. At least it led to some very important information. Let's circle back and talk about that Carol Burnett song I was searching for.

As far as I can remember, and since I can't find the lyrics online, we'll have to rely on my creaky memory. It was supposedly sung by a child about seeing the colors of the rainbow shining through a glass prism and wondering about the origins of the prism since it wasn't connected to communism or socialism or anything like that.

The point of this very convoluted explanation of an obviously very obscure song is that the things you look at in the physical world, like sunlight, can be seen in literally a different way by looking at them from a different perspective.

You can see daylight as a rainbow of colors simply by viewing it through a prism. The same is true of our emotions and the way we see them in our day-to-day lives.

Let's say we're still stuck in our old way of thinking, the one that is dominated by our subconscious. In that mode, we mostly view things through a fear, anger, and guilt triangle that can be seen as the base of that particular prism.

The emotions of fear, anger, and guilt are what I refer to as the three ugly stepsisters because they always band together and feed off one another's negativity to make our lives as miserable as Cinderella's before she met the handsome prince. And I know there are only two ugly stepsisters in that story, but just go with three for now.

Those three are the most conditional of all our emotions, and they prevent us from loving ourselves the most. For that reason, when we allow them to dominate our thoughts and actions on an everyday basis, they prevent us from being in close connection with our guides since they only deal in the unconditional.

Learning to cope with and getting rid of the bulk of your fear, anger, and guilt is an absolute prerequisite to getting in touch with your soul guides. Entire books have been written on that subject. In fact, I wrote one of them. *Clearing the Track* is available on Amazon.com.

If you still have work to do in the area of conquering your fear, anger and guilt, I recommend doing it before continuing further on your spiritual journey.

For everyone else who feels ready, let's push on.

The triangular base of the other prism we have at our disposal has unconditional love, trust, and imagination as its points. Those three things connect us more fully with our guides.

By this time, everyone should have a pretty clear understanding of the meaning of unconditional in the spiritual sense. To put it most simply, it's the elimination of all the "yeah, buts" from your everyday thinking.

You can't be in a place where you are in control of your fear, anger, and guilt if you are still using "yeah, but" to rationalize your backsliding. Unconditional means without condition. Period.

Trust is pretty much self-explanatory, but you may be a little confused about how imagination fits into this particular triad.

When we incarnate here in these physical bodies, we bring with us a wonderful human imagination that allows talented people like J. K. Rowling to create entire alternate realities in their heads and then make them come to life on the printed page and on film.

Those of us that are less well-endowed in the area of imagination can actually use the same thought processes with the help of our guides to help picture what we want our lives to be like. Perhaps more importantly, we can imagine what our feelings will be when we get to that place.

We always have these two prisms available for our use, and we can choose to use one or the other as we see fit. We can consciously decide, as we grow spiritually, to stop viewing all the emotional scenarios in our lives through the fear, anger, and guilt prism. Let's label that one P1.

When we view our lives mostly through P1, every scenario is going to make it seem like we're being victimized, put upon, purposefully hurt, or demeaned in some way.

By using the unconditional love, trust, and imagination prism (let's call it P2) to view the same emotional scenarios, we can effectively remove the "bad" feelings and look at the same scenarios as learning experiences.

Instead of immediately going into full-blown victim mode or reacting with fear, anger, and guilt, you can ask yourself, *What is this situation showing me about myself? What exactly am I supposed to be learning here?*

If the only thing you can take away is that you figured out how you don't want to be treated, it's better than becoming angry or fearful. If you run into problems knowing how you should look at any given situation, use your imagination to think, *How would my guides react to this from the perspective of unconditional love?*

Even if you don't feel you are in very close contact with your guides, they are going to jump at the chance to be in your thoughts and send you subtle messages about how to change your perspective.

Jasper just showed up in his cowboy outfit, one of his faves, twirling a big lasso. He said, "If you ask your guides for help with this, they will happily rope you in and pull you back to a place where you can view things through P2 and away from P1."

It can be just that easy if we believe it can be—and then let it happen. The problem is that when we incarnate here, it's sort of our job to make things difficult for ourselves. Otherwise, not much learning is going on—and not much progress is being made.

To sum things up, P1 and P2 are always at our disposal for use in emotional matters, and the best way to think about them is to remember the last time you had your eyes examined.

The eye doctor puts that machine on your face, starts changing the lenses, and says, "Which is clearer—number one or number two?"

If you're like me, sometimes it's hard to tell. The same thing applies here.

Until you've learned to deal with the three ugly stepsisters and moved into a more unconditional and trusting frame of mind, it's going to be a little tough to choose whether P1 or P2 gives the clearest and best view of everything going on in your life.

Fear, anger, and guilt can cloud your judgment, and using P1 can color your perceptions to enhance those negative feelings.

Once you let your guides help you view your life through P2, you begin to realize that seeing everything through P1 was holding you back from going where you really want to go.

And if anyone ever sees an old film clip of Carol Burnett singing "Whose Little Ism Is You," please send me a link so I can know I'm not completely senile just yet.

Sphincter Boy

Before we get started on the story of how Jasper came to dub me Sphincter Boy, let me just give you some idea of what sphincters actually are.

Sphincters are naturally occurring valves in the human body that are made up of muscle to keep internal body fluids from leaking out at inopportune times.

There are sphincters that control your tear ducts, stomach, gall bladder, and urinary bladder. The most famous one is the anus.

Sphincter Boy, of course, is a phrase made famous by Wayne and Garth in *Wayne's World*. They use the name to describe a very uptight, controlling guy.

I should have guessed that, owing to his fixation on pop culture, as well as knowing all the other things he likes to call me, that it would only be a matter of time before Jasper started to refer to me by that name. And I would have been right!

Not long ago, I was thinking about him, and I innocently asked why I can sometimes hear him loud and clear, but at other times, it sounds like he's shouting from the bottom of a well.

Remember that disclaimer I put at the very beginning of this book? Here is where it comes into play. I'm going to give you his answer exactly as he gave it to me. I wrote it down right away so I wouldn't forget any of his memorable response.

My relationship with Jasper has always been open and honest. Sometimes painfully so, as you're about to find out.

He said, "First of all, you're a shithead. Sometimes your head is so full of stupid shit that you can't even hear me through it. Secondly, all of you humans have a sphincter in your head that works like an asshole. Sometimes it's wide open, and sometimes it's clamped shut. When it's closed tighter than a bull's ass in fly season, I can't talk through it." He then appeared as Patsy Cline from the early 1960s, singing her big hit, "Walking after Midnight," but he changed the lyric to "I'm tired of screaming—at your sphincter."

He said, "If you can relax, let go a little, and stop being a Sphincter Boy for a few minutes, you can get better control of your brain sphincter—and two good things can happen. First, you can open it as wide as it will go, and all that stored-up shit in your head—consisting mostly of the fear, anger, and guilt you insist on holding onto—can more easily disperse itself into the universe and drift away. Second, me and my friends here on the other side will be able to talk to you like a person and not have to get hoarse from screaming at you."

Thus saith Jasper on May 12, 2017.

Many people who have read my books say, "I wish I had a guide just like Jasper."

Really? Still feel that way after reading what I just wrote about the way he talks to me at times? What you want and need is contact with your own soul guide—not anybody else's—because you tailored them before you incarnated to be exactly what you would need them to be.

So, why did I structure Jasper to be the way he is? Because I knew in advance that I would need him to be over the top just to get my attention. Sometimes, even more importantly, he can make me laugh on a daily basis.

Seriously, when I reread the message he gave me about being a shithead, I laughed almost as much as when he gave it to me in the first place. Mostly because it's true, but also because it might be considered wildly inappropriate compared to the way people think their guides are going to interact with them.

If you're expecting to hear angelic voices giving you loving messages and thoughtful direction, it may happen. You may have designed your guide to interact with you in that way.

But just in case, you have to be prepared for any approach that your guide may take to contact you because many of us choose to have our guides talk to us the way we talk to our closest friends. Obviously, that was and is my preference.

We all come here to play this game called life, and even though it has its serious and tragic moments, it really is supposed to be fun. Most people can only have a really good time if they can relax and be themselves, and that is—without a doubt—the way Jasper and I are with each other.

But back to the substance of his message. He wants me to emphasize the sphincter in all of our heads. Even though it doesn't physically exist, spiritually it can be very helpful to picture it being there.

Here is an exercise to help you envision it. Close your eyes and picture a sphincter, or a circle of muscle, on top of your head. Jasper wants me to call it an asshole, so, okay, picture an asshole on top of your head.

Then imagine relaxing the muscle completely so that things can flow in and out freely. Jasper says you should practice visualizing your sphincter opening and closing every morning before you have that daily staff meeting with your guides. It will make it much easier for them to talk with you. At Jasper's suggestion, I have what I call a staff meeting with him and whoever else would like to attend nearly every morning.

I ask Alexa to play some relaxing music or nature sounds, and then I close my eyes, picture my brain sphincter opening completely, and ask Jasper what he has to say for the good of the day.

This gives him the opportunity to point out anything he thinks I should be thinking about or give me some information to nudge me in the direction I should be going without my thoughts interfering with what he's trying to tell me.

Throughout the day, if you can think about keeping your sphincter open, it can actually allow some of your daily encounters with fear, anger, and guilt to float away before they get lodged in your head.

I've been practicing keeping my sphincter open all the time every day since I got the directive from him, and I've found it to be really helpful in maintaining my connection to him.

If you're a little squeamish about the whole asshole-on-top-of-your-head thing, try picturing a doughnut or a bagel that can open and close the hole in its center.

All joking aside, I knew the whole head-sphincter idea was important the minute I heard it. It made a lot of sense to me, and it usually worked for me. It also opened the door for Jasper to change costumes again and give me some further explanation.

For this lesson, he appeared as the farmer in the dell, replete with bib overalls and a red flannel shirt. He took me into a barn and showed me shelves that were crowded with Mason jars in pint and quart sizes as well as buckets with lids.

All the containers were labeled with positive attributes like self-esteem, self-love, self-respect, etc.

By the way, all those attributes and 49 more are in the Power of Self program offered by my friend Barb Ruhl on her website: BarbRuhlHealing.com. The program contains 52 weeks of meditations and lessons intended to give the learner a more positive personal outlook on life, so check it out.

But getting back to Jasper's lesson, the different sizes of the containers are related to how much of each attribute you left behind with your guides on the other side and how much of each you're going to be needing for your current incarnation.

Jasper explained that, according to whichever part of your personality is abundant on the other side and a little lacking here in earth—and whichever part you need a boost in for your day-to-day functioning—your guide will select that particular container from the shelves, walk over to a big old farm sink, and pour the contents down the drain.

The drain, of course, is connected to the sphincter in your head. If it's wide open, whatever your guide is pouring in there can go directly into your brain and help replenish the particular positive emotion you are currently lacking.

If your sphincter is closed, the precious liquid can only drip in slowly. That way, it will take a lot longer for your positivity level to get back to where it's supposed to be. This can help explain why some people are never short on self-esteem, self-love, or any of the other positive emotions about self, while others have those in abundance.

Whether they are aware of it or not, they keep their head sphincters open wide most of the time, and they are the lucky recipients of all the good that comes from a close connection with the other side.

During the planning stage of your life, you decided how much of each positive trait to leave behind. You also were aware that you could have access to all of that love by having a close connection to your guides. Increasing your connection means you are also increasing the availability of all that positivity.

While Jasper is still in his farmer outfit, he wants to tell us that another great example of being connected comes from the old children's song he is representing.

In "The Farmer in the Dell," the farmer takes a wife, the wife takes a child, and so on. At the very end of the song, we come to the poor, sad cheese that has to stand alone.

Jasper says that there will be times in your life when you can identify with the cheese because you feel like you're standing all alone while everybody else has a partner.

The truth is, however, that you are never alone. You may not always feel your guides near you, but you are always connected to them—even if they like to dress up as farmers.

Time Passages

Do I even have to mention what a great old song "Time Passages" is? Al Stewart, memories of the 1970s ... it's all good. It is a wonderful song, but the lyrics, for a change, really don't have much to do with the topic at hand. I just thought we could all use a little mental break by thinking about a golden oldie before we tackle the next tough subject: transitions.

If you read my previous book, *A Matter of Death and Life*, you know that *transition* is the word the other side would like us to substitute for the word *death*.

Since what we consider to be death when we're incarnated is an illusion and doesn't exist, our friends over there thought a redefinition was in order. They chose *transition* as a more accurate description of what happens when we exit the physical body we are currently occupying and return home to the other side.

We have many transitions during our earth lives, and getting the chance to experience them is one of the biggest reasons why we incarnate here in the first place.

Living a life on this planet is to be in a constant state of change. We're born, and then we transition to children, teenagers, adults, and then senior citizens—with all the learning and growing that accompany each age.

We transition from kindergarten to elementary school, high school, college, grad school, and beyond.

We transition from dating to relationships, then living together, marriage, sometimes divorce and remarriage, and sometimes widowhood.

We transition from first job, to next job, to next job, to retirement.

Our brief incarnations are really just a bundle of all our different transitions.

The only transition that we don't actually participate in on this side is the one that many people consider to be the biggest transition of all, and that is what we call *death* here on earth.

We're all eternal beings, so even though our physical bodies "die" or cease to function, our souls simply transition to the other side when that happens.

While family and friends may insist on giving your dead body an elaborate funeral with all the trappings and the inevitable weeping and wailing, you're already back home on the other side, enjoying some well-deserved R & R.

You're not even a participant in the ultimate transition of your current incarnation!

But I digress.

Life is about constant change, and perhaps more importantly, it is about coping with that change. That's why we come here.

We could choose to stay on the other side and be our ordinary eternal selves, but when the adrenaline junkie in all of us gets bored with living in perfection, we decide to incarnate here on earth to have some fun.

No matter how much and what type of "fun" we decide to write into our life plans, we always have some fallback safety measures in place to catch us if and when we fail to fulfill those plans. We may be thrill seekers, but we're not stupid.

And who is going to be holding the safety net when we take that inevitable tumble? Our guides, of course.

You wouldn't be reading this if you hadn't survived every transition in your life up to this point. We've all experienced a few that we thought might do us in, but—somehow and somewhere—we managed to find the strength to pick up the pieces and move forward.

Many people would credit god, source, creator, universe, whatever you may view as a higher power, with making it possible for them to pull it together and keep on keeping on, and that's perfectly fine.

The truth is, though, that it was your guides and their unconditional love for you that managed to get you to focus on that little beam of light that was shining through the darkness and move toward it.

Your guides, the biggest and best part of you, in my humble opinion, exist only to help you get through this earth incarnation and accomplish whatever you came here to do. Their eyes are always on the ultimate prize, so to speak, and no one in the universe has a bigger interest in helping you through all of your transitions than them.

Take some time to think about everything you've lived through in your life—even if some of it is painful to remember. Think about all the friends you've seen come and go, all the births, all the deaths, all the good times, and all the bad times.

If you're my age, it might make you say, "Damn. I've lived through a lot of shit—and yet I survived."

Even if you're younger, when you've reached whatever age you are, and your spirituality is something you're focusing on, you've lived long enough to be able to look back and see that you've been on that roller coaster we all ride through life.

Everybody here is always in a constant state of change. The way we deal with that uncertainty that comes with it makes all the difference in how we move forward in our journeys.

Some people—you might even say *most* people—have a powerful fear of change and the transitions that it can bring about in your life.

Because they are not connected to their higher selves, and they don't understand that their guides are there only to help show them the way, which is why they're called guides, they don't trust themselves to make appropriate decisions to enable them to stay on the right path.

Because they don't trust themselves, they can't trust their guides. Since your guides are an extension of you, and you of them, if you don't have trust in yourself, you can't possibly have trust in them.

Allowing, believing, and trusting. I've talked at length about these three important qualities before, but their importance can't be overstated. All three are absolutely essential to making forward progress on your spiritual journey.

Most people can get over that first hurdle of allowing that there is much more to the universe than they currently know and understand without too much trouble.

They might even come to a place of believing that soul guides exist and that they are the part of us that we leave behind on the other side when we incarnate to help us through our earth lives without too much of a strain on their credulity.

However, when it comes to actually trusting in the new beliefs you are incorporating into your everyday thinking, that's when the changes hit a major bump in the road. This part is, without a doubt, the hardest to learn when you're initially opening up to your soul guides.

Trust. Trust that they are actually there. Trust that they know you and your life plan well enough to understand what you desire out of life. Trust that they will direct you along a path that will lead you to what you want. None of it comes easily, especially if you have latent control-freak issues, like I do.

The latest way Jasper has been showing me that he knows where I want to go and has an unobstructed view of how to get there is by acting like a football coach. He wore old-timey gray sweats with five or six whistles hanging around his neck, stood in front of a chalkboard, and drew x's and o's and arrows all over the place.

I didn't understand what he was trying to get across until he explained that he was the one designing the plays that were going to get us down the field and into the end zone. He informed me that he would also be playing quarterback. My only part in all of this was to run my route, catch the ball, and do my touchdown dance.

Even though he was promising to do 90 percent of the work—and I intellectually knew he had the best overview of how to get us where we want to go—I was still having trouble letting go and letting him truly guide things. I had hit what he later explained was a "trust wall."

When we get close to reaching a goal or making a transition—so close that we can almost see and feel it coming—our trust in our guides, and by proxy in ourselves, will be tested. This is part of the game of life.

We start to doubt everything, we go off on tangents, and we wonder if we should be doing more to help ourselves—or even doing something else entirely.

We start thinking that we might be being punished for something we did or didn't do that is blocking us from reaching our goal. You can thank your background in organized religion for that one.

When we start having these feelings, we're at a point where Jasper says we need to "simma dah nah." Just stop whatever you're doing or thinking of doing, take a deep breath, and do nothing.

Actually, not exactly nothing. We're supposed to replace those feelings of doubt with a feeling of being excited because when we hit a trust wall, we are incredibly close to getting what we want—if we can just relax and let our guides do their jobs.

If someone or something else is needed to help you get over that wall, your guides will bring them or it into the scenario without you stressing about it. Trust them to make it happen and watch closely for any little sign they may be sending you.

There are no coincidences when it comes to spiritual matters. Everything is either preplanned or brought to your attention by your guides. If you trust them, they will show you the way.

In addition to having absolute trust in your soul guides knowing what is best for you and then doing it, you need to reflect on all the transitions you've already been through in your life and realize that you are a survivor.

Too often, we look back and think about all the "bad" scenarios we managed to make it through and start to feel like victims.

Even though we often slip into playing the role of victim or martyr, it's impossible for anyone to be a victim in a life they planned out in great detail before they incarnated.

Instead of slipping into that victim/martyr role we all so love to play, view your entire life as a learning experience. Think of yourself as an A+ student. You've lived through everything that has come along so far. You're not just surviving—you're thriving. You are thriving, and you are eagerly awaiting whatever might be coming down the pike next.

Get excited about change. Adopt a bring-it attitude. Think about life as driving through one of those big outdoor Christmas light displays.

They usually start out rather simply. You know, maybe a few wrapped presents and decorated trees. Maybe the partridge in a pear tree.

As you continue driving, the displays get bigger and more elaborate—until you get all twelve lords a leaping and everything that goes with it.

If you are in close connection with your guides, that's exactly how your life will be.

Just keep asking them to show you more, and they will.

In order to see more and more new things and keep moving forward, some old things are going to have to go away or end. That should be the takeaway from this chapter.

If you want to continue to grow on this spiritual journey, you have to get used to transitions and actively seek them out. Ask your guides to bring them to you.

You may be reluctant to do so, and it may feel like it sucks for some parts of your life to end, but it's all essential for enlarging your soul by learning, which is the reason you came here in the first place.

And, just like life itself, nothing ever really ends. Everything is preserved in your memory and in the record of everything you have ever experienced in every life you have ever lived at home on the other side.

Build-a-Guide Workshop

Anyone who has kids or grandkids, or who has ever been to a mall—and I think that covers just about everybody in the good, old US of A—has been in or at least seen that store where you can put together your own teddy bear or other type of stuffed animal.

You can give the toys you build different features and dress them in different outfits. The objective is to create something that you like to look at and love enough to want to cuddle with it.

When we're doing all this work on our spiritual journeys to get more closely connected to our guides, it can sometimes be helpful to go through a similar process and construct a guide that is perfectly suited to our current situation.

I really didn't have to start from scratch and put together an idea of what Jasper might look like.

He appeared to me fully formed—in a toga—and looking like the cartoon guy on the Little Caesar's pizza box. It was his "default chillin' outfit," he says. It wasn't long before he started coming through in all manner of costumes and as all kinds of people to get his points across.

Through all his shenanigans, I still recognized him as Jasper because I became used to the energy he brings with him no matter what getup he's in.

All guides are individuals, just as we all are, and all guides are tailored by you before you incarnate to have the personality and the appearance that you want them to in an effort to make it easier to recognize them when you're beginning to look for them.

In actuality, soul guides don't really have what we would recognize as specific forms on the other side. They are sort of a nebulous mist, and some people choose to see them that way even when they are incarnated.

One person I'm aware of sees her guide as a beautiful dark green mist, and she has no problem communicating with her in that form.

When I asked Jasper what he looks like in his mist form, he immediately transformed into what looked like a rainbow-colored Afro wig—no simple primary colors for Mr. Showbiz.

I know this discussion is starting to sound like a bad sci-fi movie from the 1950s, but we basically give our guides a human appearance so they don't scare the bejesus out of us when we first raise our vibrational level to a high enough point to be in contact with them.

When you get to that place where you're allowing, trusting, and believing that your guides are there, and you're ready to see and hear them, one of the first places you should go is to the Mall of the Universe and the Build-a-Guide Workshop.

The first thing you do is listen for your guides. They probably won't come to you like Jasper came in—imitating Rip Taylor and throwing around bags of confetti—so quiet your mind as much as you can, open your brain sphincter, and listen for them.

The guides say you don't have to worry that you won't be able to understand them. Before you incarnate, you decide on a language that you both will understand, sort of like the language that sometimes develops between fraternal twins.

It may even begin as more of a language of symbols or mental pictures, but however it starts out, don't spend any time worrying that you won't be able to understand each other. Your Guidespeak was put in place before you incarnated. You just have to remember it.

Once you've conquered the language barrier, you're ready to work on the appearance of your guide.

Ask yourself these questions: What sort of a look would get my attention? What about them would catch my eye? Am I more comfortable with male or female energy? What facial features would appeal to me? Would they resemble a celebrity? How would I like to see them dressed?

I think most guides, if left to their own devices, prefer to wear ancient Greek or Roman clothes. They seem to like a classic and nonthreatening look, but how they appear will be entirely up to you.

Once you're done figuring out what type of physical appearance would be most appealing to you, it's time to work on personality.

I'll give you a forewarning. Your guides' personalities are already pretty well formed before you even incarnate because they are, after all, the part of you that you leave behind. For that reason, a lot of what they are is what you aren't.

If you are mostly quiet and shy, like me, your guide is probably going to be loud and boisterous, like Jasper.

Barb is very outgoing and talkative, and as a result, her guide, Ella, is very calm and soft-spoken. Barb has to quiet herself so she can hear her.

In both cases, our guides have personalities that are almost the direct opposite of ours. When we're most connected to them, our energy sort of dovetails with theirs.

There will be exceptions to every rule, but for the majority of people, your guides' personalities will make it easier for you to notice them and pay attention.

You most assuredly don't want an American Girl doll-type of guide who looks and acts exactly like you. If that were the case, it would be almost impossible to know if it was your guide communicating with you or if you were just listening to your own thoughts.

You want and need a guide to be the yin to your yang to get the most benefit from being connected to them.

Once you have a complete picture of your guide in your mind, you can start to imagine what it would be like to interact with them. For the vast majority of us, it is easier to communicate with someone who looks like someone you might know than a complete stranger or a nebulous mist.

Once you've done all the work I just described, you will want to see and hear from them every day—so expect to see and hear from them every day. Talk to them freely and often. Don't be defined by what other people think about you. Go ahead and talk as much as you want, wherever you want.

Jasper occasionally makes me laugh out loud, sometimes at inappropriate moments. All in all, that's actually a pretty good problem to have, and at my age, people just think I'm getting senile.

After putting in all the time and effort to build a guide who you feel will be the perfect one to work with you on your spiritual journey, it's time to connect with them, play with them, and love them as they unconditionally love you.

Stop!

Jasper repeats, "You may think you have an understanding of all the things you just read in the second part of this book, but you don't! Go back and read it again—and then you can move ahead to part III. You might even graduate from lunkhead to clueless."

James Earl Jones Is Not Your Soul Guide

Before we get into some exercises and visualizations that will help you reconnect with your soul guides in the final part of this book, I'd like to go over some of the basic things you need to have a fairly good understanding of before you can fully grasp the more advanced things I'm going to be writing about.

You may have read some of them—or something like them—before, but they are such important ideas that they bear repeating.

When beginning the process of reconnecting with their soul guides, people frequently ask, "If my guides are just another part of me, and our voices are the same, how will I know it's them and not just me having crazy thoughts?"

That is an excellent question.

A lot of people in the first stages of this journey wait and want to hear a big, booming voice like James Earl Jones saying, "Noah, build me an ark," "Luke, I am your father," or some other profound statement.

Yeah, that's not going to happen.

And when it doesn't, a lot of people just give up and stop trying to make contact at all. You need to have confidence in the fact that your guides are the part of you that you left on the other side, their voice is your voice, and their thoughts are going to be very similar to your own, at least at first.

This is one of the hardest concepts for those at the beginning of their journey to understand because they are waiting for something completely different from themselves to pop into their heads when what you're going to be hearing is you.

Whatever you will be hearing, the voice is not nearly as important as listening to what the voice is saying. Hearing what they are trying to tell you is the vital first step in establishing communication and starting to build a real relationship.

Once you have established some sort of communication with your guides, even if it is rudimentary, it's important to start asking them questions.

A lot of people get hung up at that point because they don't know what to ask or how to ask it. Let me give you a few tips.

First of all, you can't ask them a "bad" question. There is no such thing. Since your guides exist only to provide you with information and guidance to help you on your journey, you can ask them anything you like.

You also can't ask them too many questions. Those of us with children and grandchildren remember the stage when they were around three years old and asked nonstop questions. Be like a three-year-old, ask as many questions as you can think of, and wait for an answer.

Your guides are living on the other side, and since there is no such thing as linear time there, they don't have any time constraints or anything more important to do than listening to you.

You're going to be asking so many questions because, like a three-year-old, you may have to ask the same question in a hundred different ways before you get the answer you're looking for.

That doesn't happen because the guides are playing games with us—even though I sometimes feel like Jasper enjoys yanking my chain. The guides live in the atmosphere of unconditional love and understanding on the other side and cannot respond to a question that is asked in any way conditionally. They also are not able to reveal too much of your life plan to you when they answer.

Let me explain.

The guides are a lot like Google because you have to put in the right search words in the right combination to get the information you're looking for. "What color is it?" is too general.

You need to ask, "Is it red? Is it white? Is it blue?" You might go through a dozen colors before you get a yes, but that's why you should never worry about asking too many questions.

One of the reasons they will not answer nonspecific questions of this type is to keep you asking more and more questions. By doing that, your trust in your guides and your connection to them improves.

However, when asking for help and guidance, the opposite applies. You have to start out with more generalized questions and then take baby steps toward the more specific ones.

If your goal is to own a Maserati, instead of asking for one, ask them to bring scenarios into your life that will allow you to learn how to get a Maserati.

Unless you're already wealthy, a lot of the lessons will have to be about making enough money to be able to afford what you want.

Ask, "What else do I need to be feeling?" or "What else do I need to be thinking before I can get what I want?"

Ask for signs and signals that will lead you to take inspired action that will help move you forward in your journey.

Ask, "What emotions do I need to feel to get closer to what I want?"

They will bring situations into your life to give you that experience. Most often, they will say that you need to develop and hold a sense of anticipation and excitement about having what you want before you get it.

Once you know and understand how great you will feel when you attain your particular goal, you are going to do whatever the guides tell you to have that emotion all the time.

To get back to the basics of talking to your guides, I'm not sure I would call the communication between you and your guides "hearing" them.

When a formed thought pops into your head, you can tell by the energy that it carries with it that it is coming from somewhere other than your own mind. Of course people always ask, how do you know what a different energy feels like?

The answer is one that a lot of people aren't going to like, and it may make some people take a step backward.

You have to know yourself well enough to understand what something that is different from yourself feels like, and it can take a lot of time and effort on your part to be able to know yourself that well.

You have to love yourself enough to what know what love coming from another source, especially one on the other side, would feel like.

If you've gotten far enough along in your spiritual journey to be interested in the subject matter of this book, you probably have developed some insights into the truth of who you really are—from a universal standpoint.

If you still need to do some work in this area, or if you haven't even gotten to a place of self-like, let alone self-love, then I heartily recommend enrolling in Barb's "The Power of Self" program that I talked about before. It gives you fifty-two weeks of meditations and insights that will allow you to gain an understanding of yourself and the power to improve the life you are already living.

Yes, that was a blatant plug for Barb's program, but if you haven't built a foundation of unconditional love and understanding for yourself—or, at a minimum, unconditional like of yourself—you're not going to be able to connect with your guides because they dwell in unconditional love and love you unconditionally.

Even if you have only gotten to a place where you can mostly like yourself, but you're not completely ready to commit to unconditionally loving yourself, your guides can help you begin to learn the emotions and feelings that will help you understand the unconditional love they have for you.

Your guides' energy is a little different than your energy because it's pure and hasn't been corrupted by the negativity of earth, but it will still feel familiar because they have been with you since your birth—even though you may not have been aware of it.

All of this information may seem a little nebulous—or even contradictory—but the thing that makes it all come together is that your guides desire that connection with you so they can help you as much as possible on your journey.

Their only reason for existing is to be with you. They will move heaven and earth, literally, if they have to, to establish the best connection possible.

The guides can help you conquer all the fear, anger, and guilt you've accumulated in this lifetime—as well as any negativity you've managed to drag along from past lives—so that you can make your experiences during this incarnation even bigger and more conducive to learning.

One of our goals when we construct our life plans before we incarnate is always to work on as much of our emotional baggage as possible to avoid carrying it with us into our next life.

Every life we live is meant to let us learn by experiencing all the different emotions we want to while we're here.

Even though we all have had many lives down through the ages, the current popular phrase YOLO—you only live once, for my fellow old people out there—is actually true in as much as this is the only life you will have in this particular time frame, with these particular circumstances on earth, in this particular body, and as this particular person surrounded by the people in your life playing the particular roles they are playing.

For that reason, your guides want to be connected to you as much and as soon as possible to show you opportunities to gain as much life experience as you can. You only live this life once.

Once you are in close contact, you may find that, like Jasper and me, your guides might have personalities that seem to be the polar opposite of yours.

Even though we are wildly different, Jasper has always felt familiar to me, which is only natural because he is just another part of me. He's been with me since my birth, of course, but after living sixty years without any direct contact, it took a while to get to know him again, which will be the case with you and your guides.

He and I are now at the point of communicating as I imagine conjoined twins do. He's always there to talk to me, I'm always there to listen, and vice versa.

In the beginning of your rediscovery process, during the early stages of reconnection, you may not have a language to share. You may have to look for clues and signs that are put there by your guide to let you know that they are there and trying to communicate.

It's not unusual for people to find random coins around the house or when they are out and about. Placing these coins is one of the things the other side does to send messages.

If it's a penny, it's most likely one of your dead people sending you the message that they are okay and are thinking of you. But if it's a dime or quarter, the guides say it's usually them giving you a sign that they are with you and trying to get in contact.

Why the difference? I guess it's just like in the physical world. Investment counselors always tell you to pay yourself first, so if your guide can slip you a quarter rather than a penny, they're going to do it.

At any rate, it's going to take some time and some building of trust before you start to learn guide language, or Guidespeak, but it will come.

In case you are worried about a security breach, you and your guide will develop a language that only the two of you will be able to understand. It will be similar to the secret language that twins sometimes develop as babies and use to talk only with each other.

No psychic will be able to listen in on your private conversations unless one of you gives them permission to do so.

I've been able to talk to many soul guides. Barb and I talk to each other's guides on a regular basis, but it's only possible because the contact is initiated by the guides involved—and never the psychic.

Jasper says, "One way to initiate your search for your guides is to picture one of those *Where's Waldo?* drawings in your mind. Somewhere among all that crap you insist on keeping in your head, your soul guide is present."

It's your job to weed through everything in there, including your thoughts about what you believe and don't believe anymore, all your fear, anger, and doubt about yourself, and all the conditional thoughts about your place in the universe.

That means eliminating the five Ws, as well as all the yeah-buts in your vocabulary.

Once you manage to do all that, and it may not be a quick and easy thing to do—in fact, it may turn into a full-time job for a while—you will be able to spot your guide, waiting patiently for you.

If you're lucky enough to have a guide like Jasper who likes to play dress-up, you can ask them to wear a red hat and a red striped scarf for easier identification.

The good news is, just like in the Waldo pictures, once you see him, you can't unsee him. Your mind's eye will go directly to him every time you look for him.

Once you've found your guides, it's imperative that you stay tapped into them. Picture them often being in the middle of all the junk in your head. See them as you want them to appear. Do anything and everything you can to hang onto that feeling you had when you made the initial contact—no matter how small or fleeting it was.

Think about them and try to open up to them as much as possible on a daily basis. Otherwise, you may lose contact and have to start looking for Waldo again.

And if you need a do-over, don't be discouraged. Your guides aren't going anywhere. They love you so much, they will wait your whole earth life to connect with you if they have to.

Once you have a steady connection, all the other stuff you were worried about in regard to who, what, and where they are will fall away.

You can only be as connected as you realize you are. Let that light bulb of understanding appear above your head and buy a clue already.

Okay, let's all take a deep breath and gather our thoughts. If you've been able to keep up with me so far, you're in a really good place. You are able to recognize your soul guide, you can feel that their energy is slightly different than your own, and you feel connected to them if not quite reintegrated.

Don't ever become complacent and expect this to become routine without working at it. This is your new job, and you don't get weekends and holidays off. You can't get lazy, especially when this is all new to you because the connection can be easily lost if you don't keep working at keeping it open.

The guides are always there, but they can only decrease their vibrational level a certain amount to come to meet us. It's up to us to constantly try to raise our positive vibrations to get to where they are.

If we continue to wallow in all of our negativity and keep dredging up all our old fear, anger, and guilt, our positive vibration becomes less and less. If that happens, we are left with no way to communicate with our guides.

Jasper told me once that our guides actually have something that looks like a gauge that measures our positive vibrational levels. They know if it's worthwhile to try and contact us.

He said, "Think about the scene from *Elf* where Santa's sleigh is grounded in Central Park because his Christmas spirit gauge is below where it needs to be to get the thing to fly."

The guides have something very similar that tells them if we currently have enough positive energy in us to raise ourselves up to meet them.

They will still be waiting patiently for us, but they're not stupid. They're not going to waste time trying to get to us if we can't get to them.

Jasper is loving this little analogy because it gives him an excuse to dress up as both Santa and an elf. Win-win for J.

In a lesson that is maybe somewhat more practical and doesn't involve any costume changes for him, he recommends adding a daily connection routine that will make contacting your guides as simple as turning on a light switch.

When most of us wake up in the morning, the first thing we do is hit the light switch so we don't stub our toes on the footboard when we stumble off to the bathroom.

He says, "Before you even get out of bed in the morning and turn on the light, turn on your guide switch for the day. It's the same as a light switch, but it opens a connection to your guides."

You wouldn't walk into a dark room without turning on the light, so don't walk blindly into your daily routine before you turn your guide switch on.

Your guides are with you to provide illumination in the form of guiding you along the life path we have chosen for ourselves, but it's up to us to make sure that light is turned on. We are the ones who have to walk the path, but the guides will light the way if we ask them to. Don't have any doubt that they will do that for us.

Of course, we always have free will and can decide not to avail ourselves of the help they can give. We can choose to sit in a box filled with our old fears and negative emotions.

Our guides will wait patiently for us to stop being stupid and turn on the guide switch again so they can get us back on track.

I know I have had my ups and downs with Jasper, but once I was reconnected and making good progress on the way to being reintegrated, I really missed him when I lost contact because I was choosing to focus on something negative and let my vibration drop to a place where he couldn't reach me.

He always waits patiently, making pizzas to pass the time. When I finally get over myself, we get back together—and it's like a love fest.

Once you feel reconnected, do everything you can to stay that way. It only takes ten minutes a day to sit quietly, close your eyes, and ask your guide how it's going.

It's not really meditation. I know because I suck at meditation, and I know a lot of you out there feel the same way I do. It's more of a contemplation. Just picture your guides as you want to see them and then talk about the events of the day—or anything new and different you are considering doing.

It can be anything at all really. Even if neither of you have much to say, it really doesn't matter. The important thing is maintaining your connection and making it stronger by using it as often as possible.

Finding a balance between your spiritual life and your everyday life can be difficult. Most of us, for a great deal of our lives, simply ignore our spiritual sides because we're too busy living our regular lives to give them a passing thought. It is essential to your overall health and well-being to find a way to integrate the two and not neglect either one.

The Elephant in the Room

I'm not big on the importance of interpreting dreams.

Some people have devoted their lives and careers to doing just that, and hundreds, if not thousands, of books have been written on the subject, so you can read up on this subject if it seems important to you.

To me, dreams represent your subconscious processing the events of the day and your life and matching all that information up with factoids it already possesses.

I used to have a recurring dream about owning a big old house that needed remodeling. I was doing all the work myself, and it seemed like I would never be able to get it finished.

I would agree with the experts and say it means that I, in the form of the house, have a lot of work to do on my life before I'm "finished."

If I have the same thought when I'm awake, do I really need a dream to reinforce the idea? Maybe yes, maybe no.

And there are all the classic dreams like having to take a test you haven't studied for or being naked in front of a group of strangers that are supposed to have deep meanings.

There is also the Freudian thing about cigars representing penises. I get all of that, and I would never disagree with the experts on what they say it all means, but I don't think every little thing you might remember from a dream has some profound interpretation.

There is a well-known phenomenon called *astral travel*. When we sleep, our souls sometimes leave our bodies and return to the other side for some positive rejuvenation.

Our transitioned friends and loved ones can come to us in while we're sleeping. Without a doubt, a dream about Grandma coming to see you is actually her stopping by to check in and let you know she's okay and thinking about you.

With all that said, I'm going to contradict myself about not believing dreams are all that important and relate an amazing dream that a friend had about soul guides.

It perfectly explains the essence of what they are and what they can do for us.

In her dream, she saw herself as a little girl in her childhood home. She opened the front door from the inside and saw an elephant standing there.

The elephant was very friendly, and they could communicate telepathically. He told the girl he was there to be with her always and to be her best friend. He also told her that she would be able to see, hear, and talk to him, but no one else would.

The girl was thrilled to have a new friend and companion, so the elephant moved into her house and started going everywhere with her.

When they went walking, the elephant told her to get on his back and ride. He said if they came to an obstacle, she should hold on tight, and he would climb over it. She would never have to worry about getting to where she wanted to go.

The elephant started to bring the girl presents, things she was secretly longing for, but she had trouble accepting them because she didn't believe she deserved them.

After a while, the other kids at school started to notice that the girl always had an elephant with her. They start asking her why the elephant was always around. They started teasing her and calling her names. They told her she didn't need a big, smelly animal around at school, and they told her to leave it at home.

Because the other kids were so mean to her, the girl started to feel awkward and different. She sent the elephant away.

After he left, she felt alone and sad. She often thought of her elephant and was sorry that he was gone.

Isn't that a great dream? I can't believe she remembered the whole thing. It reads like a children's book on the need for self-esteem.

And even though I went through that whole thing about believing dreams are random thoughts strung together, when I heard about that particular one, it sort of made me reconsider my position.

Anyway, here is my interpretation of the dream from my skeptical perspective.

The elephant, of course, represents soul guides. They are in your life from the very beginning, often presenting themselves when you are very young as imaginary playmates.

They are your closest friends and confidants. They can help you as you travel through life, especially helping you find a way to get over the many obstacles that get thrown into your path. They can even give you gifts in the form of pointing you in the right direction on your journey and bringing people you need to help you into your life.

We can see and hear them plainly in the first four or five years of life, but as we get older, we stop believing they are there. We listen to our parents or other people who tell us that all that stuff is just a fantasy—or demons and devils.

We let the voices that are around us during our earth lives drown out our inner voices, which is what we need to hear and listen to the most.

Why on earth wouldn't you want a talking elephant as your best friend? Think of all the things it could do for you. How much simpler and easier would your life be? You would never feel alone again. Who wouldn't want that?

Well, you can have all that and more without worrying about where you can find a place to buy bales of hay in bulk.

Make your soul guide your elephant. Make your soul guide your BFF. Get to know and love him or her as much as he or she loves you, which is unconditionally. That will give you the key to unlock the love you need to feel for yourself.

The guides are, after all, the parts of us that are not present in our physical bodies. The more we love them, the more they can reflect that love back to us and make us love ourselves even more.

It turns into a giant, gooey love fest that some people may not be comfortable with at first. A lot of us were taught in different ways throughout our lives that we were not deserving of love or that it was somehow bad to love ourselves.

And more than a few of us, like me, were the lucky ones who got a hefty dose of both kinds of thinking. You have to do a lot of hard work to rid yourself of those two particular nasty old programs, but it is well worth the effort. And who can help you in doing that? Your new BFF, your soul guide.

It may seem counterintuitive because we think of guides as being filled with all kinds of positive emotions, but other than unconditional love for you, the guides don't carry any other human emotions.

They're not the human part of this equation—you are. If you are experiencing anything other than unconditional love, they are acting in their role of being giant mirrors and reflecting the emotions you are currently having.

If I feel angry, bored, or frustrated, Jasper goes into his kitchen and starts making pizza until I'm over whatever is making me feel that way.

He refuses to and is incapable of participating in any human emotion other than unconditional love. There have been times when the pizza boxes have been stacked to the ceiling before I finally come out of whatever snit I'm in.

When I'm in a "mood", he'll periodically check in and say, "Really? You're still doing this? How's that working out for you?" But he stays in his kitchen until I'm ready to love both of us again.

You'd think by now I could completely avoid his "reverse time-outs," as he calls them, but I'm still a human living a human life. Fortunately, I know that—no matter how long it takes me to come out of my funk—he'll always be there waiting for me.

He has no choice, really. He is the non-incarnated part of me, and since we've reconnected, he has been a huge part of my life.

I sometimes feel a little guilty because it's relatively easy for me to communicate with him simply because he's always there. I know that so many people are struggling to connect with their guides and are having problems doing so.

By writing this book, I'm hoping many, many more people will be able to make that reconnection that I enjoy. Well, mostly enjoy.

There's nothing special about me. I just planned to do all this before I incarnated, and now it's playing out. There is absolutely no reason anyone else can't do the same thing I have done if they can allow, believe, and trust that they can.

Keep reading! As they used to say on *The X-Files*, the truth—and the answers—are out there.

The Universe Gym

If you're like me and the vast majority of people in the world, you hate to exercise. You probably also don't like to go on diets, but that is a whole different topic. Don't get me started down that road.

A lot of us who are not gym bunnies in any way still make that New Year's resolution to be healthier and get into shape. The more ambitious among us might even go so far as joining a gym.

A select few of the hardier among us might even go to the gym and attempt to exercise in the first few weeks of January.

But then reality sets in, and you start to ask yourself, "Why am I doing this?" You hate exercising. It's a waste of time anyway because you've been doing crunches for a whole week and still have a keg where your six-pack should be.

And it hurts! Personally, I am a firm believer in the "no pain, no pain" philosophy of exercise.

So, you stop going to the gym, and before long, it's back to being your old couch potato self. Fat but happy.

So, what if you have that Dunlap disease, where your belly done lapped over the waistband of your jeans? You're not posing for nude pics anytime soon.

I'll try again next year.

Is any of this sounding familiar to anyone out there? It fits me pretty much to a T, and that is the reason I don't like to be seen in a T-shirt.

The same scenario is pretty common among people who are starting out on their spiritual journeys. In the beginning, when they realize there is something more to this life than what they are experiencing and living through, they're like the athletes on *American Ninja Warrior.*

They're running up that curved wall, trying to get a handhold on the edge, and trying to pull themselves up and over the top. After a while, some will give up trying, but others will keep running and running until they finally make it.

It's the same with learning about all the things in this book, but it is especially true when trying to connect with your soul guide. Sometimes you have to keep running up that ramp, and trying harder and harder to get a handhold and make that connection, but with persistence, you will eventually get there.

But what happens after you make the connection the first time?

Just like going to the gym, you're going think, *This is so much work.* You might even feel tired and sore for a few days after your attempts at contact. This is not the time to think that you can take a few days off and then try again.

Even if you make it up the wall and connect on your first try, it doesn't mean you're done. Not even close. If you think that way, you are completely wrong.

Once you have made some sort of rudimentary connection with your guides, it has to be nurtured and encouraged to grow just like a tender young flower.

Once you know what it feels like to be connected to your guide, you can't unknow it—even if it feels a little painful on your side as your puny human mind and heart enlarge to allow the 90 percent of you that you now have contact with to begin to fill you with unconditional love.

Your evolution into becoming connected to your soul guides and actually integrated with them has begun. Resistance is futile.

There is no way you are going to go back to kindergarten and learn to draw rectangles and triangles again when you've already been through high school and know how to do geometry.

As a precaution, I would refer you back to the chapter that talks about the sphincter on the top of your head. Even though you are connected, you still have to make a daily conscious effort to keep yours open at all times.

In the morning, before my daily staff meeting with Jasper, I sometimes picture myself with an old-fashioned crank, like they used to open awnings on storefronts, sticking out of my ear. I use it to crank open my brain sphincter just to make sure it's available to Jasper in case he wants to pour any information in there.

There is another exercise that sounds like it brings more joy to Jasper than it brings to me. He says if your brain sphincter is open as much as possible, your guides may find things in your mind that you aren't worried about. They'll send you scenarios to help you cope with and alleviate those little worries before they turn into big worries.

"Just another service we provide," he says.

The things I talk about in relation to connecting to your guides may seem like a great deal of fuss and bother, and sometimes they are, but it's better to consider them a challenge than work because confronting challenges and facing them down is the primary reason we came here.

An earth life is meant to be an adventure—like going to a really great amusement park.

Very few people are going to pay the price of admission to sit on a bench and watch everybody else going on all the rides and having all the fun.

We're here to experience life—a life we could never directly know by staying on the other side—and the knowledge we gain from all of our experiences helps in the expansion and growth of the universe. We want to do more and be more, so we become more.

But I digress. We're supposed to be learning how to stretch and strengthen the spiritual muscles that connect us to our soul guides.

It all boils down to seeing the pathway to connecting to our guides less as hard work and more as an attainable natural progression in our spiritual journey. The journey often begins when you develop a knowing that something is missing from your life and a yearning to find out what it might be.

For some people, it can happen when they are young in earth years, and for others, like me, it can hold off happening until you're old and decrepit.

Age really isn't a factor when you awaken to your spiritual side, and it certainly doesn't mean that anyone is "better" than anyone else because they found their connection sooner rather than later.

All it means is that some people either had less crap to work through in this life, or they worked through it faster to get to a place of self-appreciation and high self-worth that was at or near the border of self-love that would allow you to know that a connection with your guide was even possible.

The key to unlocking that love of self that most of us are desperately searching for is to develop an unconditional love for your guide. And trust me, with a guide like Jasper, it ain't always easy.

But doing that accomplishes two very important things. It lets your guides reflect more and more of that love you're sending in their direction, and having more access to your guides actually gives you more access to yourself and all the unconditional love the universe is holding for you.

Starting to sound like some new-agey BS to you? Maybe a little. But it all comes back to believing in yourself and loving yourself.

A little while ago, Barb's guide Ella was on a kick about telling us how silly humans are. She told us that one of the silliest things we do when incarnated is putting total trust in our guides and then not trusting ourselves to believe in everything they say.

They are us. If we trust them, we are, in fact, trusting ourselves.

I have a hard time trusting myself when I know there is a box of candy in the house I shouldn't be eating, but when it comes to making life choices, I trust myself to make to the right decision for me because I've grown enough spiritually to know that Jasper is not going to give me bad advice.

He is the 90 percent of me that's on the other side. In listening to him, I trust *me* not to steer me wrong.

It certainly wasn't always that way.

Before my reconnection, I made some not-so-great decisions on my own that caused me to doubt the trust I had placed in myself to make good choices. Somehow, even in those dark times, Jasper managed to scream loudly enough in my ear to give me enough direction to keep me from going completely off the rails.

I've presented a lot of new ideas about interacting with your soul guides throughout this book, but the idea of our guides being extensions of our incarnated selves is one of the most important—and one of the hardest to wrap our puny human minds around.

The key to unlocking the power of loving yourself lies in loving your guides enough so they can reflect that love, which increases your love of them. That creates an infinite circle of increasing love on both sides because they are you and you are them.

It sounds much more complicated than it actually is.

Once you fully understand that they are the part of you that you left behind only because the totality of you is too awesomely huge to fit into a tiny human body, it becomes clearer in your puny human mind.

And how do we move toward and finally accomplish this wonderful thing, this coming together with the parts of us we had to leave behind in order to live out an earth life?

How do we actually move past mere reconnection to our soul guides and achieve reintegration?

By doing the thing I talked about at the beginning of this chapter: exercising. We have to exercise our spiritual muscles on a daily basis.

Your spiritual muscles can grow bigger and stronger without you having to experience all the stiffness and soreness that comes with exercising the muscles of your physical body.

One of the least painful ways to start flexing those spiritual muscles is to keep a mental list of all the little a-ha moments that occur throughout your day. Your first a-ha moment will come when you love your guide and yourself and feel the connection between you and know it is growing. How great does it feel to have that connection restored and reopened?

One of my daily a-ha moments is stopping to realize how absolutely awesome it is to be able to communicate with Jasper anytime I want—and to know he is there and will interact with me. Even though it's become a part of my normal daily routine to talk to him, I still take time to remind myself how amazing it is that I, an average schmuck, can do that.

It reinforces my self-esteem to know that I've progressed far enough in my spiritual journey that I am that connected.

Jasper told me that a major component of making this happen for us was finally believing it was possible. Believing it could happen allowed Jasper to make it happen. In essence, I allowed myself, in the form of Jasper, to give the gift of connection to myself.

Just as the love of our guides creates a big circle of love of self, believing that your guides are there to help you creates another big circle of you giving yourself what you want.

If you don't believe absolutely that what you want can happen for you, you won't be able to let you give it to you.

Have I lost some of you out there? I understand your confusion completely.

This was one of the hardest concepts for Barb and me to grasp in the beginning of our learning processes.

We both had the idea that our guides were separate energies or entities that lived on the other side and that we had enlisted them during our life planning to be our guides during this particular incarnation.

In fact, even after Jasper and Ella had made it abundantly clear that they were not separate entities—they were the parts of us we left behind—we still persisted in thinking that they were separate from us. We both liked the idea of someone outside ourselves coming to our rescue.

Even though we were both being Cleopatra—the queen of denial—our guides never stopped loving us, talking to us, and presenting reality whenever they could.

We finally and grudgingly accepted that Ella was, indeed, part of Barb, and Jasper was part of me.

Why did we resist facing the obvious truth for so long? I think it was for the same reason people want to see their guides as angels or other supernatural beings. It's the drama and romance of thinking some being from the other side is going to swoop in and save you from some terrible fate or perhaps something even worse: yourself.

That type of magical thinking plays into that most human of conditions: our love of being the victim. I've said it a thousand times, and I'll keep repeating it until everyone on the planet finally gets it: You can't be a victim in the life you planned for yourself.

Everything in your life was put there by you and by design for you to accomplish your learning goals. It may be that you can't get past some emotion, but that just makes you unwilling to learn and move forward. It doesn't make you a victim.

Once you fully accept that your soul guides are part of you and their personalities were designed by you to give the best fit with the personality you decided to adopt for this incarnation, your reconnection is well on its way to becoming *reintegration*.

And reintegration with our guides is the main goal. I absolutely love being in constant contact with Jasper, even when he is being a jag-off, as we say in Western Pennsylvania. It's always exciting to know that he is helping me help myself get to where I want to go.

I have reached the point where I am always asking him, "What's next?" Once you've gotten close to your current goal, you may feel the excitement that comes from striving for it fading a little. However, you always have to be ready to look for the next challenge.

A good way to think about goals is to imagine yourself on a dock and looking out to sea.

If you can see your current goal as a ship that is just about to where you are standing and preparing to tie up, then look out at the horizon and see that the ship carrying your next goal is out there and heading for port. Then put on your guide goggles and spot the next one heading your way.

And the next one.

And the next one.

See a whole string of ships lined up and coming into the harbor.

It's less important that you know what each ship is carrying and more important that you know all the ships are there and heading in your direction.

Thinking about reaching your goals in this way accomplishes two things.

First, it stresses the importance of having goals and thinking big. You may think reaching an individual goal is important, and it is, but it's equally as important to realize that reaching a goal is just a stepping-stone to reaching the next goal.

Secondly, it can force you to believe in the grandness of your life and yourself by realizing that your current incarnation is so big that the ocean is full of ships just carrying your dreams to you.

All controlled by self.

You have to believe that you are the only one who can bring what you want to yourself by using your soul guides to help you accomplish just that.

Once you truly know that you—and only you—are in control of your life, then take that control and use it. Ask your guides directly to help you, and they will.

They are incapable of lying, unlike us when we are incarnated, and they will let us know when we are doing something stupid.

They will definitely call BS on you because they don't deal in it. They are communicating directly from the unconditional atmosphere of the other side, so listen carefully to what they have to tell you.

There's Never a Bridge Too Far

In the 1960s and 1970s, there were a lot of movies about World War II that involved bridges.

I guess it was because as the Nazis blew up a lot of bridges in Western Europe as they were forced to retreat into Germany. Some very old and historically important bridges were blown up in an attempt to slow the advancing Allies.

According to Wikipedia, the Allies tried to capture bridges over the Rhine River between the Netherlands and Germany in 1944 before the Nazis could destroy them. It spawned a book that was turned into a Hollywood blockbuster movie in 1977: *A Bridge Too Far*.

"A bridge too far" was a term credited to one of the generals who was involved in the planning of the operation and the postmortem held to figure out what had gone wrong. The term has seeped into the English language and is defined by the Oxford dictionary as "a step or act that is regarded as too drastic to take."

What does this little lesson in military history from the 1940s have to do with our spiritual journeys? More than you might think.

Jasper uses old movies to teach us about how to use our guides to help us along the way. In this instance, he's using the title of *A Bridge Too Far* to tell us that the concept of an action being too drastic to take may apply to some of our earthly endeavors, but it is absolutely not true when it comes to spiritual advancement.

There are no steps that would be too drastic if you're truly interested in moving forward, raising your vibration, and becoming more closely connected to your guides. The only exception being if you feel a need to hurt yourself or others, you've gone too far.

The fear of something seeming too radical to change can slow or even stop our forward progress. Depending on how deeply connected you are to your old programs, even the thought of making a change can send you running for cover.

If you find yourself in a situation where the fear of change is stronger than the desire to change, you've slipped out of allowing, believing, and trusting that your guides are there to help you. Don't forget that they possess the information to keep you moving forward on the correct path.

Jasper suggests thinking of temporary setbacks as ravines on the path of your spiritual advancement.

You want to keep moving forward, and you're pretty sure you want to take the straightest path possible to make your journey shorter and easier, but there doesn't seem to be any way across to the other side of the canyon.

This impediment to your progress represents your fear of change or your fear of the unknown.

Depending on the size of your fear, it can appear as a simple ravine, the Grand Canyon, or something in between. No matter the size, fear is still fear, and the only way to get over it is to use the help available from your guides to build a bridge.

You do that by believing and trusting that a bridge is going to be there to support you when you ignore your fear and take a step forward.

Your fear probably isn't going to go away completely, but it can be managed to the point of you being able to ignore it completely. You will be able to take one small step at a time on the bridge you have allowed your guides to put in place for you.

I'm afraid of heights, and Jasper enjoys watching me struggle at times. He likes to call it "tough love."

When he was showing me this analogy, the bridge appeared as one of those rickety wooden ones made out of planks that are spaced out far enough that you can see down between each step.

He said he used that type of bridge so I would stop looking down at my fears and look straight ahead at the goal I was moving toward. Also, he said managing and conquering your fears builds character.

He also thought it was hilarious to make me nervous about the crossing when I should have absolute trust that he would get me across safely.

I told him that I thought it was borderline sadistic behavior, but that just made him laugh harder.

I hope you put more empathy into your guide than I did into mine when I was designing him.

Anyway, the best way I have found to get over your fears is to bring back our old friend Glinda the Good Witch and have her wave her magic wand at your fear and say, "Be gone—you have no power here!"

The Glinda reference has worked well for me, but if you're getting tired of it, here's a line from another great movie that may be more to your liking.

In *The King and I,* Deborah Kerr sang, "Whenever I feel afraid, I hold my head erect and whistle a happy tune so no one will suspect I'm afraid." Look at the third stanza of that song: "The result of this deception is very strange to tell, for when I fool the people I fear, I fool myself as well!"

There it is, folks. In 1956, legendary lyricist Richard Rogers revealed one of the secrets of the universe in a movie—and a musical no less.

Since your fears of this nature are not based in any kind of reality, the way to get rid of them is to fool your subconscious into thinking you are not afraid of them anymore.

Convincing your subconscious that all emotional fears are fake is a complicated topic that will be covered in my next book. For now, you can make do by pretending you have no fear. You can do that by calmly walking over the bridge that has been placed there by your guides, regardless of its condition.

You're probably asking, *What was I thinking at the beginning of this lesson? Once I get over the ravine and arrive on the other side, I've reached my goal, right?*

As usual, Jasper gets to push that big red button to make that annoying "eh" sound and say, "Wrong!"

You may have gotten past that particular fear, but once you get to the other side, you come to a landing at the bottom of a flight of stairs. As you look up the stairs, you see that they lead to other bridges, other platforms, and many more flights of stairs.

I had expected, as I'm sure many of you will, that once I got to the other side of whatever fear I was working on conquering, I was done. I had arrived. My personal goal had been met.

J was only too happy to do his Beatles impression (he somehow manages to be all four of them at the same time) and launch into a rousing version of "Day Tripper" to remind me that this is not a once-and-done thing.

I am not a day tripper, and neither are you.

By choosing to learn how to increase our spirituality, we've committed to go on a journey that will last for the rest of our current earth lives. Since we can't bring 100 percent of who we really are into these human bodies we inhabit without our heads exploding, we are driven to keep learning as much as we can to maybe get that needle on our spiritual fuel gauge up to 20 percent.

Imagine how spiritually aware we would all be if we could double the amount of our true universal selves that we carry around in our puny human minds!

The goal is to use our guides to provide us bridges to get us across and up the next flight of stairs to a better understanding of who and what we are in a spiritual sense.

Letting our guides do their job and actually guide us also gives us a feeling of being more in control of our lives because we know they are the biggest and best part of who we are.

By allowing us to help ourselves and grow in knowing we have the ability to do just that, we get closer to being in total reintegration with our guides.

Jasper wants us to go back to the movies—he would have us live at the movies if it were possible—and your favorite Harry Potter film.

Whenever we get to where we think we want to be, or whenever we think we've achieved whatever goal we thought we were shooting for, there may be a landing, but there will always be another set of stairs.

And just like the stone stairways at Hogwarts, your set of stairs may move and attach themselves to another landing—even while you're still climbing them.

You may arrive at a platform you were not expecting to be on and wonder where you are. Rest assured that it is the correct one for the place you are in your journey because it is the one your guides have directed you to.

Your guides are holding the grand plan for your current incarnation, and they know how and where to direct you to stay on that plan even if you thought you were heading somewhere completely different.

Instead of being afraid when you see an obstacle in the path of your spiritual journey, consider it a good sign. It means you've changed enough to have gotten control of whatever fear the obstacle represents. It means you're ready to deal with it and move ahead.

When you start to get a feeling that change is coming, even if you are not sure what it might be, you should put your guides on alert and start asking them to build that bridge over the obstruction and help you see it and get across it.

Once you get used to feeling the change in your emotions from negative to positive when you get close to needing a bridge to cross, you're going to actually start craving them. You'll be actively asking your guides to bring you new experiences and show you signs that can help you move toward them.

That brings a closer connection to your guides, which leads to more integration with them.

Jasper has just one more movie analogy, and then he promises no more—at least not in this chapter.

Guidespeak

If you saw *Avatar*, you will remember the scene where the native people take the ends of their long hair braids and integrate them with the hair of their flying animals. He says that is a great example of how you can integrate with your guides—minus the intertwining long hair.

Between humans and our guides, it's strictly a mental picture, but it achieves the same result. You and your guides start to think as one, and you move forward together. You supply direction, and they supply the wing power to get you there.

Into the Woods

Jasper is going to let us leave the cineplex (for a short time, I'm sure) and let us go outside for a walk in the woods. This exercise is not really like a movie because you're going to have to use your imagination to see it rather than having it play out on a screen.

Imagine you are walking on a flat path that feels safe and winds through a beautiful field of wildflowers until you come to the edge of a forest.

The path splits into four separate paths that veer off in different directions, but they all end up going into the forest. The trees are just dense enough that you can't tell where any of the paths go after entering.

In the distance, on the other side of the forest, you can see a mountain with a clearing on the top. Instinctively, you know that the mountain is your ultimate destination, and it's going to be your goal to get there.

You feel so attracted to the mountain because your guides are up there in that clearing. Looking down from their perches, they can see how all the paths wind through the forest and any obstacles that might be blocking them. All the paths converge at the base of the mountain.

It really doesn't matter which path you choose to take through the forest because they all end up at the same place, which is ultimately where you want to be. Your guides can see all the paths, direct your journey, and keep you on the path you picked if you trust them to do so.

Some of the paths may be more contorted than others, and some may have more pitfalls and be a little more "dangerous" than the others, but following any of them will ultimately get you where you want to go.

The important thing to remember is that no matter which path you choose, your guides have an overview of the entire forest and everything you will encounter. They will be there to help you every step of the way, using the knowledge they hold from both your life plan and from being up in their observation post.

Using just your normal human senses, you're never going to be able to work up the courage to choose one of the paths and plunge forward into the forest.

It looks dark in there. It's scary. There might be lions and tigers and bears, oh my! Sorry, Jasper promised to leave the movies behind, but when an opportunity presents itself, he can't help himself.

There might be bandits. There might be big potholes or trees down across the road, blocking the way.

Countless bad things could happen.

Our imaginations run rampant when we are using only our five physical senses to make decisions about moving into the unknown.

The subconscious mind dredges up every fear it can find lying around in your memory because it will use any means to make us stay where we are and be safe. After all, we're in a nice, flat, open field of beautiful wildflowers. Not much harm can come to us if we just stay put.

Luckily, for those of us experiencing the spiritual inertia that comes with these moments of indecision, there is a very nice park bench at the place where our current path ends and the four new ones begin. We decide to sit down for a few minutes and think about our predicament.

After sitting for a while, and still being unable to make a decision about which path to take, you notice two objects on the bench.

One object is a really nice set of noise-canceling headphones, and the other is a blindfold that looks like the big black kind that Dorothy Kilgallen and Bennett Cerf used to put on during the mystery guest segment of *What's My Line?* Wow, did I just date myself! If none of the words in the last part of that sentence made any sense to you, you're going to have to fire up Mr. Google!

When you've conquered enough of your fears, developed enough trust in your guides to feel that you're ready to move forward, and are ready to let go of your control issues enough to allow your guides to pick the best path for you, they are going to want you to put on those fancy new headphones.

Jasper, of course, wants me to call them "Jasper-phones," but you can use whatever name feels right to you.

By putting them on, you cancel out all the negative noise you may be hearing from friends and family and have your guides' voices directly in your ear. That way, it's much easier to hear the advice and direction they are giving you.

Next comes the blindfold. Jasper says this whole exercise is starting to sound like a sequel to *Fifty Shades of Grey*. I knew he couldn't stay away from the movie references for very long.

Putting on the blindfold—at least for control freaks like me—is much more difficult than putting on the headphones.

With the headphones and the blindfold, you become completely dependent on your guide to tell you which way to go on the next part of your journey. It's the ultimate test of your trust in them, and it makes perfect sense when you think about from their perspective.

Are you going to rely on your own very limited vision and hearing just because that's what you've been doing all your life—or are you going to trust the guidance of someone who can see the entire path in front of you and knows what you had planned to encounter along the way? Do you want to stick with what you know and are comfortable with just because you have a deep need to always be in control instead of giving the biggest and best part of you the control?

If that is the way you want things to be, you better just stay on that bench because all you are doing is inviting more grief and heartache. That's how you've been living up to that point. How has that been working out for you? Obviously not all that well if you're reading this book in an attempt to improve your life.

You have to know and believe to your very core that your guides, being just another part of you, are going to lead you in the right direction and then trust them to do that.

Jasper says, "Imagine walking along the path you've chosen and coming to a deep ravine. The only way across is balancing on a narrow board that has been placed over it. With your eyes open, there is no way you are going to be brave enough to be like one of the Flying Wallendas and tiptoe across."

However, with your blindfold on—and your guide holding your hand and telling you where and how to place each step—you can get across easily and continue on your journey.

It gives a little twist to the definition of blind faith, doesn't it? At any rate, the important thing to do is to stop paying attention to your current reality. If your reality is having to balance on a board to get over an obstacle, it's best to ignore it, put on your blindfold, and ask for help from your guide.

If it helps you understand how your guides see a much clearer picture than you, think of that 10 percent of the bigger you that currently occupies your physical body as a corrupted computer program.

Your subconscious and your friends, family, and acquaintances are like computer viruses, constantly trying to infect your hard drive with the negativity they carry to keep you from changing and moving toward more positivity.

It's like the old story about why they never have to put a lid on a barrel of live crabs at the fish market. If one crab tries to crawl out of the barrel, all the other crabs will grab it and pull it back down. None of them are able to escape. A similar thing happens among humans when they decide to change their way of thinking about their spiritual selves.

Most of the people around you, and even your own subconscious, are going to do everything they can to keep you exactly where you are because they are happy and comfortable with you there—even if you are not happy and comfortable with yourself. They are not ready for or interested in changing, and they don't want you to either.

For that reason, you start looking at things more and more from the virus's point of view.

Fortunately, our guides, living and dealing only in the unconditional, have the ultimate hard drive cleaner, and by looking toward the future and listening only to them, they can help you eliminate all the viruses that are making up your current reality and allowing you to run smoother—just like a new computer.

Obviously, we're all here to live out our earth lives, and we have to deal with the reality around us on a daily basis, but leave your headphones and blindfold on as much as is practical.

You can never have too much exposure to your guides, and focusing as much as possible on them will lessen the focus on your current reality.

The Victory Lap

In an earlier chapter, I wrote about the transitions we all go through in the various stages of our earth lives.

When we are here and incarnated, we tend to think of transitions more as endings than as changes, which is what they actually are.

Because we are eternal beings, when we are at home on the other side, there is nothing we can experience that would be called an ending. Everything is always moving, changing, and expanding, but because nobody ever "dies" and there is no such thing as linear time, there are no endings.

That's one of the things that makes living out an earth life so attractive to us. It's a chance to experience what endings feel like. In fact, on earth, we can't have a new beginning without some sort of ending.

The emotions surrounding those kinds of scenarios can be painful and sucky, but we all have to learn to move on from our various endings because learning to cope with those emotions gives us the greatest amount of learning and enables our soul growth.

That brings me to the point of this chapter. Without a doubt, the biggest and most frequently asked question about life from spiritual seekers and everyone else is: *Why? Why do we come here? Why would we put ourselves through all this heartache and suffering? Why would we choose this kind of life if we had the chance not to?*

The sort of stock answer up until now has been the one I wrote about at the beginning of this chapter. We're here to experience the things we can't when we're living in the pure, positive atmosphere of unconditional love on the other side so that we can learn and ultimately enhance the growth of our souls and the entire universe.

All of that is true, even though it sounds a bit nebulous and timeworn.

I believe to my core that we come here to help our souls enlarge, but I always thought that was a kind of simplistic and not too sharply defined explanation. I always thought there had to be more to it.

In a recent session with Barb, Jasper and Ella finally gave us a new component that occurs during our transitioning from an earth life back to the other side to explain more fully one of the major reasons we incarnate. It's called the *victory lap*.

I wrote at length about everything we encounter when we go home to the other side after living an earth life in *A Matter of Death and Life*, and I'm not going to go over it again in great detail here.

I want to focus on the part soon after we transition back.

That's when we're reviewing the life we just led with our guides and counselors and doing some preliminary thinking about what we will choose to focus on in our next life.

The guides had always told me that it was a review where you could see your entire life, not flashing before your eyes, but in great detail so that you could evaluate each and every scenario and determine what, if anything, you had learned.

That does happen, but after sitting through all of that, what occurs next is what Jasper calls the "victory lap."

You're not driving a race car around a track with a checkered flag hanging out the window, though I guess you could do that if you really wanted to. You're actually in a special room with a big round table that exists only for the purpose of you being able to tell everyone assembled everything that you are proud that you accomplished during your just-lived life.

The locals call it the "bragging room" because that's what you get to do there.

You get to talk about how good it felt to conquer whichever negative emotions you dealt with this time around, and everybody there will be excited to hear what you have to say.

Here on the earth plane, those of us raised in a Christian tradition were always taught that pride goeth before a fall, but once we get home, pride goeth a long way in making us feel good about living through another incarnation and learning everything we learned.

That is where the payoff comes for people who chose to live through a lot of difficult situations and persevered.

They can brag about surviving and still thriving and be given praise by everyone in attendance. That's part of the reason why some people choose such "hard" lives: to be a hero in the bragging room.

You don't want to get to the other side and only be able to say, "Well, I got married and had a couple of kids, and I went to work, and then I died."

That may sound like a typical life, but that's only going to get you a pat on the head and maybe a small trophy for participating. You want to receive adulation—like you have just won a gold medal in an Olympic event.

Because with all the praise and admiration comes a lot of positive vibrational energy, which leads us to the other thing that happens in the bragging room.

After you've described all the wonderful things you accomplished during your earth life, your positive vibrational level is assessed so that a determination can be made about what emotional scenarios you will be able to choose for your next life.

If you're the guy who got the participation trophy, chances are you didn't choose to work on many of your issues. You're going to end up living a life similar to your last one.

Playing it safe during an earth life doesn't do much to increase your growth and learning, and it leads to a lot of coulda, shoulda, wouldas in the bragging room when you're supposed to be talking about all the things you accomplished.

If there is little to no increase in your positive vibration, there won't be much difference between your next life and the one you just finished, but you will be given more negativity to deal with so you can better see the contrast between what you want and what you don't want.

The universe is always growing and expanding, and it needs each and every one of us to contribute to that growth and expansion by learning to deal with the emotional scenarios we choose for ourselves in each of our earth lives.

Ultimately, that is the reason for this book.

As the emotional atmosphere of earth becomes more negative over time, our connection to our soul guides and the help they can give us to get us through an earth life becomes increasingly important.

I hope the information I have been able to provide—as supplied by Jasper, Ella, and a few other souls over there—helps everyone who reads this book have a reconnection that leads to total integration with their guides.

Preview of The Blueprint

Up until now, my books have usually had one big theme: my personal spiritual journey, death and life, the law of attraction, or soul guides.

Lately, I've been getting so much information from my personal soul guide, Jasper, on a variety of topics that I decided to do something different. I am covering several diverse but related topics in one book.

The title of the work is *The Blueprint*, and it starts out by describing the blueprint we all come into our earth lives with. It allows us to distinguish ourselves from rocks and trees and from each other.

After that, I'm going to delve into human fears: how they are divided into two groups, how they evolved from our earliest days in tribal societies, and how to deal with them on a spiritual level.

Next will be a discussion of how our roots in those early tribal societies still affect us today and how to find your tribe in your current life.

The next topic will be one I'm really excited about. "The Deal" is a new initiative from the other side that gives a different perspective on using your spirit guides to bring what you want into your life.

I'll also be relating anything else that might be revealed in the meantime.

Jasper just showed up as the genie from *Aladdin* and sang, "You ain't never had a friend like me." He is so right. I never know where his lessons are going to take me in my spiritual journey, so stay tuned and I'll give you an update in *The Blueprint*.

CPSIA information can be obtained
at www.ICGtesting.com
Printed in the USA
BVHW08*0934270818
525723BV00005B/24/P